50 Innovative & Disruptive Companies

Daniel Boyd

DEDICATION

To the trailblazers, risk-takers, and visionary leaders who defy convention, challenge norms, and reshape our world through innovation and disruption.

This book is dedicated to the extraordinary companies that have dared to dream big, break boundaries, and transform industries. Your relentless pursuit of excellence and unwavering commitment to pushing the limits inspire us all.

Table of Contents

ACKNOWLEDGMENTS

Writing a book like "50 Innovative and Disruptive Companies" is a collaborative effort that would not have been possible without the support and contributions of many remarkable individuals. As I reflect on this journey, I would like to express my deepest gratitude to those who have made a significant impact:

To the dedicated teams and employees of these companies, your passion, hard work, and unwavering commitment to excellence are the driving forces behind their success. Your contributions to shaping industries and embracing innovation are invaluable.

To my family and friends, thank you for your unwavering support, understanding, and encouragement throughout the entire writing process. Your belief in me and this project fueled my determination to bring it to fruition.

With heartfelt appreciation,
Daniel

0. Introduction

Innovation is the lifeblood of progress and the driving force behind transformative change. Throughout history, certain companies have risen above the rest, captivating our imaginations and redefining entire industries with their groundbreaking ideas, audacious visions, and relentless pursuit of excellence. This book, "The Innovation Chronicles: Inspiring Tales of Trailblazing Companies," invites you on a captivating journey into the world of these remarkable organizations.

Within these pages, you will delve into the stories of fifty innovative companies that have reshaped the business landscape and left an indelible mark on our society. From tech giants that have revolutionized the way we communicate and access information to visionary startups that have disrupted traditional markets, each company has a unique tale of ingenuity, resilience, and unwavering commitment to pushing the boundaries of what is possible.

Through vivid narratives and compelling anecdotes, we will explore how these trailblazers took bold risks, defied conventional wisdom, and triumphed in the face of adversity. From the early days of humble beginnings to their meteoric rise to prominence, you will witness the birth of groundbreaking technologies, the birth of new industries, and the birth of global movements that have forever changed our world.

"The Innovation Chronicles" goes beyond mere success stories. It delves into the core of what makes these companies truly innovative and examines the key strategies, principles, and mindsets that have propelled them to greatness. You will discover how they harnessed cutting-edge technologies, disrupted traditional business models, embraced sustainability and social responsibility, and fostered cultures of creativity, collaboration, and relentless pursuit of customer satisfaction.

As you embark on this inspiring journey, you will witness the power of human ingenuity and the extraordinary impact that innovative companies can have on our lives. Whether you are an aspiring entrepreneur, a seasoned business leader, or simply a curious reader eager to learn from the best, "The Innovation Chronicles" promises to ignite your imagination, spark your own innovative spirit, and empower you to embrace the endless possibilities that lie within the realm of innovation.

1. 23andMe

23andMe is a fascinating journey that began with the vision of two remarkable individuals and their drive to empower people with knowledge about their own DNA. Founded in 2006 by Linda Avey, Paul Cusenza, and Anne Wojcicki, 23andMe set out to revolutionize the way individuals understand and engage with their genetic information.

Anne Wojcicki, a biologist and entrepreneur, played a pivotal role in shaping the company's direction. Inspired by her own experiences and the belief that access to genetic information could have a profound impact on healthcare and personal well-being, Wojcicki co-founded 23andMe with the goal of making genetic testing and personalized health insights accessible to everyone.

The company's name, 23andMe, reflects the 23 pairs of chromosomes that make up the human genome. At its core, 23andMe aimed to provide individuals with a deeper understanding of their genetic ancestry, health predispositions, and traits through direct-to-consumer genetic testing.

In its early days, 23andMe faced numerous challenges. The company needed to develop affordable and reliable DNA testing kits, establish partnerships with reputable laboratories for processing the samples, and navigate the complex landscape of regulatory requirements for genetic testing.

Through perseverance and innovation, 23andMe made significant strides. The company developed a simple and user-friendly saliva collection kit that customers could easily use at home. By sending their DNA samples back to the 23andMe laboratory, individuals could gain access to a wealth of genetic insights, ranging from ancestry composition and genetic health risks to carrier status for certain inherited conditions.

One of the key factors that set 23andMe apart was its focus on engaging customers beyond the initial testing experience. The company built a robust online platform where users could explore their genetic data, participate in research studies, and connect with others who shared similar genetic traits or ancestry. By encouraging customers to contribute their data for research purposes, 23andMe amassed a vast database that has been instrumental in advancing scientific understanding of human genetics and uncovering genetic associations with various traits and diseases.

However, 23andMe faced regulatory hurdles along the way. In 2013, the U.S. Food and Drug Administration (FDA) issued a cease-and-desist order, raising concerns about the accuracy and interpretation of health-related genetic tests offered by the company. This led to a temporary suspension of 23andMe's health-related genetic testing services.

Undeterred, the company worked diligently to address the FDA's concerns and restructured its offerings to focus on ancestry and genetic genealogy while working toward regaining FDA approval for health-related reports. Over time, 23andMe expanded its range of offerings and introduced new features, such as wellness reports and traits analysis, to enhance the value it provided to its customers.

In recent years, 23andMe has continued to innovate and evolve. The company has forged partnerships with pharmaceutical companies and researchers to leverage its genetic database for drug discovery, clinical trials, and advancing precision medicine. In addition, it has expanded its international presence, bringing genetic testing and personalized insights to individuals around the globe.

The story of 23andMe is one of perseverance, scientific curiosity, and a relentless commitment to empowering individuals with knowledge about their own DNA. By harnessing the power of genetics and building a vibrant community, 23andMe has played a significant role in transforming the field of direct-to-consumer genetic testing, revolutionizing personalized healthcare, and contributing to groundbreaking scientific discoveries.

2. Adobe Systems

The story of Adobe Systems is a tale of innovation, creative vision, and pioneering software solutions that have transformed the way we create, communicate, and experience digital content.

The roots of Adobe can be traced back to 1982 when John Warnock and Charles Geschke, both former Xerox researchers, founded the company. Their goal was to develop software that would enable the seamless exchange of documents across different computer systems, which was a significant challenge at the time.

One of Adobe's earliest breakthroughs came in the form of the PostScript page description language, developed by Warnock. PostScript revolutionized the printing industry by enabling high-quality, device-independent printing and was widely adopted by printer manufacturers. This technology laid the foundation for Adobe's future success.

In 1985, Adobe released its first commercial product, Adobe Illustrator, which quickly became a game-changer for graphic designers. Illustrator was one of the first vector-based drawing programs, allowing users to create scalable artwork that could be resized without losing quality. It became a staple tool for design professionals and set the stage for Adobe's dominance in the creative software market.

Adobe's next major milestone came in 1989 with the release of Adobe Photoshop. Developed by Thomas Knoll and his brother John Knoll, Photoshop was a groundbreaking image editing software that introduced features like layers and filters, revolutionizing digital image manipulation. Photoshop became synonymous with photo editing and has remained an industry standard for more than three decades.

As the internet gained popularity in the 1990s, Adobe recognized the need for web-focused tools. In 1996, the company acquired FutureWave Software, which had developed a vector-based animation program called FutureSplash Animator. Adobe rebranded it as Adobe Flash and transformed it into a platform for creating interactive multimedia content on the web. Flash became ubiquitous and played a significant role in shaping the early days of online experiences.

In the early 2000s, Adobe continued its expansion through strategic acquisitions. Notably, in 2005, Adobe acquired Macromedia, a leading multimedia software company. This acquisition brought popular software products like Dreamweaver for web development and Flash Player into Adobe's portfolio, solidifying its position as a dominant force in the creative software market.

As technology advanced, Adobe recognized the growing importance of digital documents and the need for efficient document management. In response, the company developed Adobe Acrobat, a software suite for creating, editing, and sharing PDF (Portable Document Format) files. PDF quickly became a universal standard for digital document exchange, ensuring document integrity and compatibility across different platforms and devices.

Adobe's transition to a subscription-based model with the introduction of Adobe Creative Cloud in 2013 marked another significant milestone. This shift allowed users to access Adobe's suite of creative software through a subscription service, providing regular updates and enhanced collaboration features. The Creative Cloud subscription model proved successful and fostered greater accessibility for both professionals and aspiring creatives.

Over the years, Adobe has continued to innovate and expand its product offerings. It has introduced applications like Adobe Premiere Pro for video editing, Adobe InDesign for desktop publishing, and Adobe XD for user experience design. The company has also focused on integrating its software with cloud-based services and advancing technologies such as artificial intelligence and machine learning to enhance creative workflows and automate tedious tasks.

Today, Adobe is a global leader in digital media and marketing software, providing a comprehensive suite of tools that empower creatives, marketers, and businesses worldwide. Its software is used by millions of professionals across industries, from graphic design and video production to web development and digital marketing.

The story of Adobe Systems is one of relentless innovation, visionary leadership, and a commitment to empowering creativity in the digital age. By continuously pushing the boundaries of what is possible, Adobe has played a transformative role in shaping the way we create, communicate, and engage with digital content.

3. Airbnb

Airbnb is a remarkable tale of turning a simple idea into a global hospitality phenomenon. It all began in 2007 when two roommates in San Francisco, Brian Chesky and Joe Gebbia, were struggling to afford their rent. With a major design conference coming to the city, they saw an opportunity to offer visitors an alternative to overbooked hotels. They decided to rent out three air mattresses in their apartment and provide breakfast to their guests, thus giving birth to the concept of "Air Bed and Breakfast."

To help bring their idea to life, Chesky and Gebbia were joined by their former roommate, Nathan Blecharczyk, who had expertise in computer science and served as the technical mind behind their venture. Together, they launched a simple website that allowed hosts to list their available space and guests to book accommodations.

In the early days, Airbnb faced numerous challenges and struggled to gain traction. To fuel growth and overcome the initial resistance from potential users, the founders personally reached out to hosts in cities where major events were taking place, offering to help them create listings and attract guests. This hands-on approach helped establish trust and grow the Airbnb community organically.

The turning point came in 2008 when the founders attended the Democratic National Convention in Denver. They realized that traditional accommodations were in short supply, and their platform could provide an affordable and unique solution. The success of the event marked a pivotal moment for Airbnb, with increasing numbers of hosts and guests joining the platform.

As Airbnb expanded globally, the founders encountered regulatory challenges and resistance from the traditional hospitality industry. Some cities and municipalities had strict regulations regarding short-term rentals, and Airbnb had to navigate a complex landscape to comply with local laws and regulations. The company collaborated with governments and introduced tools to address concerns, such as the collection of lodging taxes and the implementation of safety measures.

Over time, Airbnb expanded its offerings beyond air mattresses to include entire homes, apartments, treehouses, castles, and even unique experiences hosted by locals. The platform's emphasis on authenticity, personalized experiences, and the sense of belonging created a new paradigm of travel, connecting people from different cultures and backgrounds in a way that traditional accommodations could not.

In 2011, Airbnb reached a major milestone by securing $112 million in funding, valuing the company at $1 billion and marking its entry into the coveted unicorn club. The funding allowed Airbnb to invest in technology, expand its global presence, and refine its user experience.

The company continued to innovate and introduce new features to enhance the platform. They introduced a robust review system, enabling guests and hosts to provide feedback and build trust within the community. They also focused on improving the user interface, mobile app experience, and customer support to ensure seamless transactions and positive experiences for users worldwide.

In 2020, Airbnb faced unprecedented challenges due to the global COVID-19 pandemic. Travel restrictions and lockdowns severely impacted the travel industry, including Airbnb's business. However, the company quickly adapted and responded to the crisis by promoting local and domestic travel, implementing enhanced cleanliness protocols, and introducing flexible cancellation policies to address the changing needs and concerns of guests and hosts.

Since its humble beginnings, Airbnb has experienced exponential growth and disrupted the hospitality industry on a global scale. The platform has provided opportunities for millions of hosts to monetize their extra space, while offering travelers a unique and authentic way to explore new destinations. Today, Airbnb is a household name and a trusted platform for millions of users, spanning more than 220 countries and regions worldwide.

The story of Airbnb showcases the power of entrepreneurship, community, and the sharing economy. By embracing the spirit of innovation, leveraging technology, and fostering human connection, Airbnb has transformed the way we travel and opened up a world of possibilities for both hosts and guests, redefining the concept of hospitality along the way.

4. Alibaba

Alibaba had an entrepreneurial vision, paired with perseverance, and technological innovation that has revolutionized the e-commerce landscape in China and beyond. Founded in 1999 by Jack Ma and his team of 17 colleagues in Hangzhou, China, Alibaba began as a small startup with a grand ambition—to connect businesses and consumers through the power of the internet.

Jack Ma, a former English teacher, had a unique vision for Alibaba. He recognized the untapped potential of the internet in China and envisioned a platform that would empower small and medium-sized enterprises (SMEs) to thrive in the digital age. He named the company "Alibaba" after the famous folk tale "One Thousand and One Nights," which represented a world of limitless possibilities.

In its early years, Alibaba faced numerous challenges. China's e-commerce ecosystem was still nascent, and the concept of online shopping was unfamiliar to many. Moreover, the dot-com bubble had burst, leading to widespread skepticism about internet-based businesses. However, Jack Ma and his team persevered, driven by their unwavering belief in the transformative power of the internet.

Alibaba's first breakthrough came with the launch of Alibaba.com, an online marketplace that connected Chinese manufacturers with international buyers. By providing a platform for SMEs to showcase their products and reach a global audience, Alibaba.com helped level the playing field and democratize trade for businesses of all sizes. The platform rapidly gained popularity, and Alibaba expanded its services to include business-to-business (B2B) and business-to-consumer (B2C) transactions.

In 2003, Alibaba introduced Taobao, a consumer-to-consumer (C2C) online marketplace that aimed to capture the domestic e-commerce market in China. Taobao quickly gained traction by offering a wide range of products, competitive prices, and robust customer protection measures. To overcome the lack of trust in online transactions, Taobao implemented an escrow payment system that withheld funds until buyers confirmed receipt of goods, ensuring a safe and reliable shopping experience.

In 2004, Alibaba faced a significant challenge when eBay, a global e-commerce giant, entered the Chinese market. The competition between Taobao and eBay was fierce, but Alibaba's relentless focus on understanding the local market, adapting to Chinese consumer preferences, and offering a more localized and cost-effective platform allowed Taobao to emerge as the clear winner. By 2006, eBay shut down its operations in China, cementing Alibaba's dominance in the Chinese e-commerce landscape.

Alibaba continued its expansion with the launch of Tmall in 2008, a business-to-consumer platform that allowed brand owners and authorized merchants to sell their products directly to Chinese consumers. Tmall focused on providing a premium shopping experience, emphasizing trusted brands, quality assurance, and customer service. Tmall became a go-to destination for Chinese consumers seeking authentic and high-quality products.

In 2014, Alibaba made history with its initial public offering (IPO) on the New York Stock Exchange. It became the largest IPO in history at the time, raising over $25 billion and valuing the company at approximately $231 billion. The IPO brought Alibaba to the global stage, showcasing the scale and potential of China's e-commerce market.

Building upon its e-commerce success, Alibaba diversified its portfolio and expanded into various sectors. It launched Alipay, a digital payment platform, which later became Ant Group, offering a range of financial services. Alibaba also ventured into cloud computing, artificial intelligence, logistics, entertainment, and more, establishing itself as a leading player in the broader digital economy.

Today, Alibaba Group is a global technology conglomerate with a vast ecosystem of platforms, services, and subsidiaries. It encompasses e-commerce platforms (Alibaba.com, Taobao, Tmall), digital payment systems (Alipay, Ant Group), cloud computing (Alibaba Cloud), logistics (Cainiao), media and entertainment (Alibaba Pictures, Youku), and much more.

The story of Alibaba is a testament to the transformative power of innovation, the potential of the internet, and the perseverance of its visionary founder, Jack Ma. By empowering SMEs, enabling consumer trust, and revolutionizing the way people shop, Alibaba has reshaped the e-commerce landscape, propelled China's digital economy, and emerged as a global leader in technology and innovation.

5. Amazon

Amazon is a story of relentless ambition that has reshaped the way we shop, read, entertain, and even compute. From its humble beginnings as an online bookstore to its current status as one of the world's largest and most influential companies, Amazon's journey is a testament to its founder, Jeff Bezos, and his unwavering commitment to customer-centricity and long-term thinking.

In 1994, Jeff Bezos, a former Wall Street executive, set out to capitalize on the rapid growth of the internet by establishing an online bookstore. He chose the name "Amazon" after the largest river in the world, envisioning a company that would become a vast and diverse marketplace. Operating from his garage in Bellevue, Washington, Bezos launched Amazon.com as an online bookseller, initially offering a selection of one million titles.

In its early years, Amazon faced significant challenges. The e-commerce industry was still in its infancy, and many skeptics doubted the viability of online retail. However, Bezos and his team remained focused on their mission to provide customers with an unparalleled shopping experience, offering a vast selection, competitive prices, and convenient delivery.

Amazon's breakthrough came in 1995 when it expanded beyond books and began selling a wide range of products, including electronics, music, and movies. The company's success was fueled by its relentless pursuit of customer satisfaction, exemplified by its customer reviews, personalized recommendations, and efficient logistics infrastructure.

To sustain its growth, Amazon embraced technological innovation. In 1997, the company went public, raising capital to fund its expansion plans. Over the years, Amazon introduced numerous groundbreaking initiatives and services that redefined the retail landscape. In 1999, it launched "Amazon Prime," a subscription service that offered free two-day shipping on eligible items, setting a new standard for fast and convenient online shopping.

The early 2000s marked a period of diversification for Amazon. It expanded its product categories, introduced new marketplaces in different countries, and acquired companies like Zappos, an online shoe retailer, and Audible, an audiobook platform. In 2007, Amazon disrupted the technology industry with the launch of the Kindle e-reader, revolutionizing the way people read and paving the way for the digital publishing revolution.

One of Amazon's most significant transformations came with the introduction of Amazon Web Services (AWS) in 2006. Initially conceived as an internal infrastructure service to support Amazon's own operations, AWS evolved into a cloud computing platform that revolutionized the IT industry. By offering scalable and cost-effective computing power, storage, and other cloud services, AWS became a dominant force, serving businesses of all sizes worldwide.

As Amazon expanded its reach, it prioritized customer convenience and introduced innovative services such as Amazon Prime Video, a streaming platform for movies and TV shows, and Amazon Echo, a smart speaker powered by the voice assistant Alexa. The company also made a bold move into the grocery industry by acquiring Whole Foods Market in 2017, further expanding its physical presence.

Amazon's commitment to innovation has extended beyond retail and technology. In 2013, Bezos unveiled a long-term vision for

Amazon called "Prime Air," aiming to revolutionize package delivery using autonomous drones. While still in development, this ambitious project exemplifies Amazon's relentless pursuit of innovative solutions to improve the customer experience.

Today, Amazon is a global behemoth, operating in numerous industries, including e-commerce, cloud computing, digital entertainment, artificial intelligence, and more. It has redefined customer expectations, disrupted traditional retail models, and established itself as a leader in innovation and customer obsession.

However, Amazon's success has not been without controversy. The company has faced criticism for its labor practices, market dominance, and impact on small businesses.

Nonetheless, its influence on the global economy and its ability to anticipate and adapt to changing consumer behaviors cannot be denied.

The story of Amazon is a testament to the power of relentless innovation, customer-centricity, and long-term thinking. From an online bookstore to a global conglomerate, Amazon's journey reflects the transformative nature of the digital age and serves as a symbol of entrepreneurial success and audacious ambition.

6. Apple

Apple has transformed the consumer electronics industry and redefined the way we interact with technology through its innovative federation of hardware and software design, by discarding norms of what we think of for many common consumer electronics. Founded in 1976 by Steve Jobs, Steve Wozniak, and Ronald Wayne, Apple started as a humble startup in a garage in Cupertino, California.

The company's early years were marked by the release of the Apple I and Apple II computers, which gained popularity for their user-friendly interface and unique design. However, it was the introduction of the Macintosh in 1984 that catapulted Apple into the spotlight. The Macintosh was the first commercially successful computer to incorporate a graphical user interface and a mouse, revolutionizing the way people interacted with computers.

Despite early success, internal conflicts led to Steve Jobs' departure from Apple in 1985. The following years were challenging for the company as it faced increasing competition and declining market share. However, in 1997, Apple made a pivotal decision by bringing Steve Jobs back as CEO. Under Jobs' leadership, Apple embarked on a journey of innovation and reinvention that would shape the company's future.

One of Apple's most significant turning points came with the launch of the iMac in 1998. The iMac was a breakthrough product that combined cutting-edge design with powerful performance. Its colorful and translucent casing challenged the traditional notion of what a computer should look like and captured the imagination of consumers. The iMac's success revitalized Apple and set the stage for a series of game-changing products.

In 2001, Apple introduced the iPod, a portable digital music player that revolutionized the way people listened to music. With its sleek design, user-friendly interface, and integration with iTunes, the iPod became a cultural icon and propelled Apple's resurgence. The subsequent release of the iTunes Store in 2003 further disrupted the music industry by providing a legal and convenient platform for purchasing and downloading digital music.

In 2007, Apple unveiled the iPhone, a revolutionary smartphone that combined a mobile phone, an iPod, and an internet communicator in a single device. The iPhone's multi-touch interface, elegant design, and robust ecosystem of apps transformed the mobile industry and sparked a smartphone revolution. Subsequent iterations of the iPhone introduced new features and technologies, solidifying Apple's position as a leader in mobile innovation.

Building upon its success, Apple expanded its product lineup to include the iPad, a tablet computer that redefined the way we consume media and interact with content. The iPad's intuitive touch interface and vast selection of apps made it a game-changer in the tablet market, creating a new category of devices.

In addition to hardware, Apple ventured into software and services. In 2008, the company launched the App Store, an online marketplace that revolutionized the distribution of mobile applications. The App Store empowered developers to create innovative and diverse apps, fueling the growth of the iOS ecosystem.

Apple's commitment to design excellence extended to its computers as well. In 2008, the company introduced the MacBook Air, a slim and lightweight laptop that set new standards for portability and aesthetics in the industry. Subsequent iterations of the MacBook and iMac continued to showcase Apple's emphasis on sleek design, powerful performance, and seamless integration of hardware and software.

Under the leadership of Tim Cook, who succeeded Steve Jobs as CEO in 2011, Apple expanded its reach into new markets and services. The company introduced Apple Pay, a mobile payment system, and Apple Watch, a smartwatch that combined health and fitness tracking with digital connectivity. Apple's focus on privacy and security also resonated with users, positioning the company as a trusted steward of personal data.

In recent years, Apple has placed a greater emphasis on services such as Apple Music, Apple TV+, and Apple Arcade, further diversifying

its revenue streams and leveraging its ecosystem of devices.

Today, Apple is one of the world's most valuable and influential companies, with a devoted customer base and a reputation for creating products that seamlessly blend technology and design. Its annual product launches have become highly anticipated events, generating buzz and setting trends in the tech industry.

The story of Apple is a testament to the power of visionary leadership, relentless innovation, and a commitment to creating products that delight and inspire. From computers to music players, smartphones to wearables, Apple has consistently pushed the boundaries of what is possible, shaping the way we live, work, and connect in the digital age.

7. Baidu

Baidu has shaped the landscape of internet search and services in China. Founded in 2000 by Robin Li and Eric Xu, Baidu emerged as the dominant search engine in China and has since expanded its offerings to become a comprehensive internet company with a wide range of products and services.

Robin Li, a Chinese computer scientist, recognized the need for a search engine that could effectively navigate and index the Chinese language and content. This led to the development of Baidu, which launched its search engine in January 2000. Baidu's early years were challenging, as it faced intense competition from global search giants like Google and Yahoo.

However, Baidu's breakthrough came with its focus on understanding the unique needs of the Chinese market and tailoring its services accordingly. The search engine implemented algorithms and technologies specifically designed for the Chinese language, including support for Chinese characters and localizing search results. Baidu also prioritized partnerships with Chinese content providers to ensure relevant search results for its users.

As Baidu gained popularity, it expanded its offerings beyond search. In 2004, the company introduced Baidu Baike, a Chinese-language online encyclopedia similar to Wikipedia. Baidu Baike allowed users to create and edit articles, fostering a collaborative knowledge-sharing platform.

In 2006, Baidu launched Baidu Tieba, an online community platform that allowed users to create and participate in forums on various topics. Baidu Tieba became one of the largest online communities in China, enabling users to connect, share information, and engage in discussions.

Baidu's growth continued with the introduction of additional services. It launched Baidu Zhidao, a question-and-answer platform, which quickly became a popular resource for users seeking advice and information. Baidu Maps, a mapping and navigation service, was also introduced, providing users with accurate and detailed maps of China.

In 2009, Baidu expanded into the online video market with the launch of Baidu Video (now iQiyi), a leading video streaming platform in China. iQiyi offers a vast library of licensed and original content, including movies, TV shows, and variety programs, and has become a major player in China's entertainment industry.

Recognizing the growing importance of mobile, Baidu invested heavily in mobile search and services. In 2012, it released the Baidu Mobile app, providing users with a seamless and optimized search experience on mobile devices. Baidu also ventured into mobile payments with the launch of Baidu Wallet, offering users a convenient and secure way to make payments and transfers.

Baidu's commitment to innovation extended to emerging technologies. The company invested in artificial intelligence (AI) research and development, establishing Baidu Research in 2011. Baidu has made significant advancements in AI, particularly in natural language processing, computer vision, and autonomous driving.

However, Baidu faced challenges and controversies along the way. The company has faced criticism for allowing the promotion of misleading medical information in its search results and has been subject to government regulations regarding online content and advertising practices.

Nonetheless, Baidu remains a key player in China's digital landscape, with its search engine commanding a significant market share. The company continues to expand its offerings, diversifying into areas such as cloud services, smart devices, and autonomous driving technologies.

The story of Baidu reflects the importance of understanding local markets, adapting to user needs, and leveraging technological innovation to establish a leading position in the competitive internet industry. Through its search engine and a wide range of services, Baidu has become an integral part of the daily lives of millions of Chinese users, shaping the way they access information, connect with others, and consume digital content.

8. Beyond Meat

Beyond Meat is a company synonymous with culinary innovation that has revolutionized the plant-based food industry. Founded in 2009 by Ethan Brown, Beyond Meat set out on a mission to create delicious, plant-based alternatives to traditional animal-based meat products, with the goal of positively impacting human health, animal welfare, and the environment.

Ethan Brown, a former clean energy executive, recognized the urgent need to address the environmental and health challenges associated with animal agriculture. Inspired by the potential of plant-based proteins, Brown assembled a team of scientists, engineers, and chefs to develop a breakthrough technology that could replicate the taste, texture, and appearance of meat using only plant-based ingredients.

After years of research and development, Beyond Meat introduced its flagship product, the Beyond Burger, in 2016. The Beyond Burger is made primarily from pea protein isolate and other plant-based ingredients, carefully engineered to mimic the juiciness and meaty texture of traditional beef burgers. The product gained immediate attention for its ability to satisfy meat lovers' cravings while being entirely plant-based.

One of the key innovations of Beyond Meat was its focus on

creating a more sustainable food system. The company aimed to reduce the environmental impact of meat production by minimizing water usage, land requirements, and greenhouse gas emissions associated with animal agriculture. By sourcing plant-based ingredients, Beyond Meat sought to offer a more environmentally friendly alternative to traditional meat consumption.

Beyond Meat's success did not go unnoticed. In 2019, the company made headlines when it went public on the NASDAQ stock exchange, becoming the first plant-based meat company to do so. The initial public offering was met with significant enthusiasm from investors and consumers alike, highlighting the growing demand for sustainable and plant-based food options.

Building on its early success, Beyond Meat expanded its product lineup to include a variety of plant-based meat alternatives. This included Beyond Sausage, Beyond Beef, and Beyond Chicken, catering to different culinary preferences and allowing consumers to incorporate plant-based options into their favorite dishes. The company also partnered with major foodservice chains and retailers to make its products widely available to consumers across the United States and internationally.

Beyond Meat's commitment to innovation and continuous improvement led to further advancements in its product offerings. The company focused on enhancing the nutritional profile of its products, reducing saturated fats, and increasing protein content. Additionally, Beyond Meat expanded its research and development efforts to explore new plant-based protein sources and optimize its manufacturing processes.

The impact of Beyond Meat extends beyond the plant-based meat alternatives it offers. The company's success has helped fuel a larger movement towards plant-based eating, inspiring other entrepreneurs and established food companies to invest in the development of alternative protein products. Beyond Meat's innovations have prompted conversations about sustainability, animal welfare, and the future of food.

While Beyond Meat's journey has been marked by achievements and widespread adoption, it has also faced challenges and criticism. Some argue that plant-based alternatives should not be seen as direct replacements for traditional meat but rather as complementary options. The company has also faced competition from other plant-based meat producers and traditional meat companies launching their own plant-based offerings.

Nevertheless, Beyond Meat has undoubtedly made a significant impact on the food industry, pushing the boundaries of what is possible with plant-based ingredients and challenging the status quo of meat consumption. Its story showcases the potential of innovation and entrepreneurship to drive positive change in the way we produce and consume food, offering a glimpse into a more sustainable and compassionate future.

9. BYD Company

BYD Company is a story of environmental sustainability, and global success. Founded in 1995 by Wang Chuanfu, BYD (Build Your Dreams) started as a small battery manufacturer in Shenzhen, China.

Wang Chuanfu, an engineer and entrepreneur, recognized the potential of electric vehicle (EV) technology and set out to develop advanced rechargeable batteries for a wide range of applications. BYD initially focused on producing rechargeable batteries for mobile phones and soon became one of the leading battery suppliers in China.

However, BYD's breakthrough came in 2003 when it shifted its focus to electric vehicles. Recognizing the growing global demand for sustainable transportation solutions, BYD invested heavily in research and development to create its own electric vehicle technologies, including batteries, powertrains, and charging infrastructure.

In 2008, BYD introduced its first electric vehicle, the BYD F3DM (Dual Mode), a plug-in hybrid sedan. This was followed by the launch of the all-electric BYD e6 in 2010, which gained popularity as a reliable and efficient electric vehicle. BYD's commitment to technological innovation and product quality quickly earned the company recognition and accolades in the automotive industry.

BYD's success in the electric vehicle market was further solidified by strategic partnerships with global automakers. In 2009, Warren Buffett's Berkshire Hathaway invested in BYD, recognizing the company's potential and its position in the rapidly growing EV market. The partnership with Berkshire Hathaway provided BYD with the financial stability and global reach to expand its operations and reach a wider audience.

BYD's technological advancements extended beyond electric vehicles. The company diversified its product portfolio to include energy storage systems, solar panels, and electric buses. BYD's electric buses, in particular, gained significant attention and popularity around the world. By combining its expertise in battery technology and electric drivetrains, BYD became one of the world's largest manufacturers of electric buses, providing sustainable transportation solutions for cities and reducing carbon emissions.

In addition to its success in the automotive and energy sectors, BYD also ventured into other industries, such as consumer electronics and rail transportation. The company's commitment to sustainable development and clean technology drove its expansion into these areas, offering innovative products such as electric forklifts, energy-efficient home appliances, and monorail systems.

BYD's dedication to environmental sustainability has been a core principle of the company since its inception. By promoting the adoption of electric vehicles and renewable energy solutions, BYD aims to reduce carbon emissions and combat climate change. The company's efforts in this area have earned it recognition and numerous awards for its contributions to environmental protection.

Beyond its domestic success, BYD has expanded its global presence and established a strong foothold in international markets. The company has established manufacturing facilities and research centers in various countries, including the United States, Brazil, Hungary, and India, allowing it to serve customers worldwide and contribute to local economies.

The story of BYD is a testament to the power of technological innovation, visionary leadership, and a commitment to sustainability. From its humble beginnings as a battery manufacturer, BYD has evolved into a global leader in electric vehicles, energy storage, and renewable energy solutions. With its continued focus on clean technology and sustainable development, BYD aims to shape the future of transportation and contribute to a greener and more sustainable world.

10. Coupang

Coupang is a captivating tale of e-commerce innovation, rapid growth, and entrepreneurial tenacity. Founded in 2010 by Bom Kim, a Harvard Business School graduate, Coupang has emerged as one of South Korea's most prominent and successful online retail platforms.

Bom Kim recognized the immense potential of e-commerce and sought to create a company that would revolutionize the way people in South Korea shopped for everyday goods. With a vision to provide customers with fast and convenient delivery services, he established Coupang with the goal of becoming the "Amazon of South Korea."

Coupang differentiated itself in the market by implementing a unique business model centered around a "Rocket Delivery" service. This service aimed to offer customers same-day or next-day delivery of their orders, ensuring an exceptional shopping experience. To achieve this ambitious goal, Coupang built an extensive logistics network and developed innovative delivery solutions, including its own fleet of vehicles and a proprietary algorithm to optimize the delivery process.

In the early years, Coupang faced numerous challenges, including fierce competition from established players in the e-commerce industry and logistical complexities associated with fast delivery. However, the company's relentless focus on customer satisfaction and its commitment to operational excellence helped it gain traction and attract loyal customers.

Coupang's breakthrough came in 2013 when it launched its "Rocket Wow" service, which offered guaranteed same-day or next-day delivery on a wide range of products. This service not only set Coupang apart from its competitors but also propelled the company to rapid growth and popularity among South Korean consumers.

To further enhance its offerings, Coupang expanded into additional product categories, including electronics, beauty, fashion, and groceries. The company also invested in advanced warehouse automation technologies to improve efficiency and speed in order processing. Coupang's commitment to quality and customer satisfaction earned it a reputation for reliability and convenience, solidifying its position as a leading e-commerce platform in South Korea.

In 2014, Coupang raised significant funding from international investors, including SoftBank Vision Fund, securing the resources needed to fuel its expansion plans. The company used the funds to further develop its logistics infrastructure, enhance its mobile app and website, and expand its product selection.

Coupang's growth trajectory continued in 2018 when it introduced its own private-label brand, Coupang Basics, offering a range of high-quality, affordable household products. This move allowed Coupang to further control its supply chain and offer exclusive products to its customers.

The company's innovation and success caught the attention of global tech giants, leading to significant partnerships and investments. In 2020, Coupang secured a strategic partnership with Walmart, which acquired a minority stake in the company. This partnership provided Coupang with access to Walmart's global supply chain expertise and expanded its reach in the international market.

In March 2021, Coupang made headlines by going public on the New York Stock Exchange in one of the largest initial public offerings (IPOs) by a South Korean company. The IPO catapulted Coupang's market value to tens of billions of dollars, further cementing its status as a major player in the e-commerce industry.

Today, Coupang continues to innovate and expand its services. The company leverages technology, data analytics, and AI-driven algorithms to enhance its delivery capabilities and personalized shopping experiences. Coupang's commitment to customer-centricity and relentless pursuit of operational excellence has enabled it to thrive in a highly competitive market, transforming the way people in South Korea shop online.

The story of Coupang serves as an inspiration to entrepreneurs and showcases the power of disruptive thinking, technological innovation, and unwavering dedication in building a successful e-commerce business.

11. DeepMind

DeepMind is on the cutting-edge artificial intelligence research, groundbreaking discoveries, and the pursuit of solving complex problems using machine learning algorithms. Founded in London in 2010 by Demis Hassabis, Mustafa Suleyman, and Shane Legg, DeepMind has emerged as a world-leading AI research company, pushing the boundaries of what is possible in the field of artificial intelligence.

Demis Hassabis, a former child chess prodigy and neuroscientist, had a vision of developing AI systems that could simulate human intelligence and solve some of the world's most challenging problems. He assembled a team of talented researchers and engineers, bringing together expertise from various fields, including computer science, neuroscience, and mathematics.

DeepMind gained early recognition for its achievements in machine learning and reinforcement learning, two areas of AI that focus on training algorithms to learn and make decisions based on feedback from their environment. The company's breakthrough came with the development of a neural network algorithm called Deep Q-Network (DQN) in 2013. DQN demonstrated remarkable success in playing classic Atari video games, surpassing human-level performance in many instances.

In 2014, DeepMind gained international attention when it was acquired by Google, now a subsidiary of Alphabet Inc. The acquisition provided DeepMind with the resources, infrastructure, and access to vast amounts of data needed to accelerate its research and development efforts. This partnership also allowed DeepMind to collaborate with top researchers and experts within Google and further expand its capabilities.

DeepMind's research has produced groundbreaking achievements in various domains. In 2016, AlphaGo, an AI program developed by DeepMind, made headlines by defeating the world champion Go player, Lee Sedol. This historic victory demonstrated the ability of AI to master complex strategy games that were previously considered challenging for computers due to the sheer number of possible moves.

Building upon the success of AlphaGo, DeepMind continued to make advancements in AI research. In 2018, the company introduced AlphaZero, an algorithm capable of learning to play complex games, including chess, shogi, and Go, without any prior human knowledge. AlphaZero demonstrated unparalleled performance, quickly surpassing existing state-of-the-art AI systems and providing new insights into the potential of AI for problem-solving.

DeepMind's research is not limited to games. The company has also focused on applying AI to healthcare and scientific research. In collaboration with healthcare institutions, DeepMind developed algorithms to assist with the diagnosis and treatment of medical conditions, including detecting eye diseases and predicting acute kidney injury. These efforts aim to leverage AI to improve patient outcomes and revolutionize healthcare practices.

DeepMind's commitment to ethical considerations and responsible AI development is also noteworthy. The company established an ethics board to ensure that its research aligns with principles of fairness, transparency, and accountability. DeepMind actively engages with policymakers, academics, and industry experts to address the societal implications and challenges posed by AI.

The story of DeepMind represents the immense potential of AI to transform industries, solve complex problems, and drive scientific progress. Through its groundbreaking research, the company continues to push the boundaries of what is possible in the realm of artificial intelligence, with the ultimate goal of creating AI systems that benefit humanity and address some of the world's most pressing challenges.

12. Didi Chuxing

Didi Chuxing is an inspiring narrative of entrepreneurial ambition, technological disruption, and rapid growth in the transportation industry. Founded in 2012 by Cheng Wei, Didi Chuxing has become one of the world's largest and most influential ride-hailing platforms, transforming the way people in China and beyond travel and commute.

Cheng Wei, a former employee of Alibaba, recognized the need for a more efficient and reliable transportation system in China. Inspired by the success of ride-hailing platforms like Uber, he set out to create a similar service tailored to the Chinese market. With a vision to improve urban mobility and reduce congestion, Cheng Wei founded Didi Dache, which later merged with Kuaidi Dache to form Didi Chuxing.

The company initially focused on providing taxi-hailing services through its mobile app. Didi Chuxing aimed to leverage technology to connect passengers with available taxis, offering a convenient and hassle-free way to book rides. The service gained quick popularity among Chinese consumers, who embraced the convenience and reliability of the platform.

However, Didi Chuxing's story truly took off when it expanded its services beyond traditional taxis. Recognizing the potential of private car services, Didi Chuxing introduced private car-hailing options, allowing private car owners to offer rides to passengers through the platform. This expansion created a disruptive shift in the transportation industry, providing an alternative to traditional taxi services and meeting the growing demand for convenient and affordable transportation.

To fuel its expansion and compete against global ride-hailing giants, Didi Chuxing secured significant investments from prominent technology companies and investors, including Tencent and Alibaba. These investments provided the company with the financial resources needed to scale its operations, develop new technologies, and expand its market reach.

Didi Chuxing's commitment to innovation led to the introduction of additional services and features. The company launched carpooling services, enabling passengers traveling in the same direction to share rides, reducing congestion and promoting resource efficiency. Didi Chuxing also invested in research and development of autonomous driving technologies, aiming to transform the transportation industry further.

In 2016, Didi Chuxing made a strategic move by acquiring Uber's China operations, effectively ending the fierce competition between the two ride-hailing giants. This acquisition solidified Didi Chuxing's dominance in the Chinese market, allowing the company to expand its services and user base.

Beyond ride-hailing, Didi Chuxing diversified its offerings to include other mobility solutions. The company introduced bike-sharing services, allowing users to rent bicycles for short-distance commuting. It also ventured into car rental, chauffeur services, and smart transportation systems, further establishing itself as a comprehensive mobility platform.

Didi Chuxing's growth and success have not been without challenges. The company faced regulatory hurdles, particularly related to passenger safety and driver qualifications, leading to stricter regulations imposed by Chinese authorities. In response, Didi

Chuxing implemented enhanced safety measures, including driver background checks and real-time monitoring, to ensure the safety of passengers using its platform.

With its rapid expansion and increasing influence, Didi Chuxing has expanded its operations beyond China. The company has entered into partnerships with international ride-hailing platforms, expanding its global presence and serving customers in various countries.

The story of Didi Chuxing embodies the transformative power of technology and entrepreneurship in shaping the transportation landscape. By leveraging mobile technology, data analytics, and innovative business models, Didi Chuxing has disrupted the traditional transportation industry, providing millions of people with accessible and convenient mobility solutions. As Didi Chuxing continues to evolve and expand its services, it remains at the forefront of the ride-hailing revolution, pushing the boundaries of what is possible in urban transportation.

13. DJI

DJI (Dà-Jiāng Innovations Science and Technology Co., Ltd.) is a leader in the rise of consumer drones. Founded in 2006 by Frank Wang, a young entrepreneur from China, DJI has become the world's leading manufacturer of unmanned aerial vehicles (UAVs) and aerial photography systems.

Frank Wang, who had a passion for remote-controlled aircraft from a young age, recognized the potential of drones as a transformative technology. He saw an opportunity to create high-quality, user-friendly drones that could capture breathtaking aerial images and videos. With this vision in mind, Wang established DJI in his dorm room at Hong Kong University of Science and Technology.

DJI initially focused on producing flight controllers and drone accessories for enthusiasts and hobbyists. However, the company's breakthrough came in 2010 with the introduction of the DJI Phantom, a ready-to-fly quadcopter equipped with a built-in camera. The Phantom series revolutionized the consumer drone market, making aerial photography and videography accessible to a broader audience.

The Phantom's success propelled DJI into the global spotlight, attracting attention from photographers, filmmakers, and aerial enthusiasts worldwide. The company's commitment to innovation and product quality, combined with its intuitive user interface and stability, set DJI apart from its competitors. The Phantom quickly became a bestseller, solidifying DJI's position as a leader in the consumer drone industry.

DJI continued to innovate and expand its product line. The company introduced the Inspire series, targeting professional photographers and filmmakers, offering advanced features such as interchangeable lenses and high-resolution cameras. These drones were designed to capture stunning aerial footage with exceptional stability and precision.

DJI's commitment to pushing the boundaries of drone technology was evident with the launch of the DJI Mavic series in 2016. The Mavic Pro, a foldable and highly portable drone, introduced unprecedented convenience and versatility to aerial photography. The Mavic Pro's compact size and advanced features, including obstacle avoidance and intelligent flight modes, made it a game-changer in the industry.

Beyond consumer drones, DJI expanded into commercial applications. The company developed specialized drones for industries such as agriculture, construction, surveying, and public safety. These drones allowed professionals to gather data, conduct inspections, and monitor remote areas more efficiently and cost-effectively than traditional methods.

DJI's success in the consumer and commercial drone markets led to collaborations with other industries. The company partnered with Hasselblad, a renowned camera manufacturer, to integrate high-quality cameras into its drones, further enhancing the aerial imaging capabilities. DJI also collaborated with thermal imaging specialists to develop drones for search and rescue operations and firefighting.

While DJI's rise has been meteoric, the company has faced challenges along the way. Concerns over drone safety, privacy, and regulatory compliance have arisen as drone usage expanded. DJI has responded by implementing geofencing technology, which restricts drones from flying in prohibited areas, and by working closely with aviation authorities worldwide to ensure responsible and safe drone operations.

Today, DJI dominates the global drone market, with a diverse range of products serving consumers, professionals, and industries. The company's commitment to research and development, technological innovation, and a user-centric approach has enabled it to maintain its market leadership and shape the future of drone technology.

The story of DJI showcases the power of entrepreneurship and technological innovation in driving a nascent industry to new heights. From humble beginnings, DJI has become a global brand synonymous with high-quality drones and aerial imaging. As the world's appetite for drones continues to grow, DJI remains at the forefront, pushing the boundaries of what is possible in aerial technology and revolutionizing the way we capture and experience the world from above.

14. Dropbox

The story of how Dropbox became a transformative company in storage, and on the frontier of cloud storage is an inspiring tale. Founded in 2007 by Drew Houston and Arash Ferdowsi, Dropbox has revolutionized the way people store, access, and share their files and documents.

The idea for Dropbox was born out of Drew Houston's personal frustration with keeping files in sync across different devices and the limitations of traditional file-sharing methods. Drawing from his own experiences, Houston envisioned a seamless and intuitive solution that would allow users to access their files anytime, anywhere.

Houston and Ferdowsi, both graduates of the Massachusetts Institute of Technology (MIT), embarked on a mission to create a file storage and synchronization service that would simplify the way people interacted with their digital content. They launched Dropbox as a private beta version, initially targeting tech enthusiasts and early adopters.

Dropbox's breakthrough came in 2008 when the company released a video showcasing the simplicity and functionality of the product. The video went viral, generating significant interest and demand for Dropbox. Within hours of the video's release, thousands of users signed up, eager to experience the convenience of cloud storage.

In 2009, Dropbox officially launched to the public, offering users a free storage plan with the option to upgrade for additional storage capacity. The company differentiated itself from competitors by focusing on a user-friendly interface, seamless file synchronization, and robust data security measures. Dropbox allowed users to effortlessly sync their files across devices, ensuring they had access to their data from desktops, laptops, smartphones, and tablets.

Dropbox's user-centric approach and commitment to simplicity and reliability resonated with users worldwide, fueling its rapid growth. The company continually expanded its features and capabilities, introducing file sharing and collaboration tools, as well as integrations with popular third-party applications. This made Dropbox not just a storage solution but also a comprehensive productivity platform.

In the early years, Dropbox faced competition from tech giants like Google and Microsoft, which launched their own cloud storage services. However, the company managed to maintain its competitive edge by focusing on its core principles of ease of use, cross-platform compatibility, and user satisfaction.

Dropbox's success attracted significant attention from investors and venture capitalists. The company secured substantial funding, allowing it to invest in infrastructure, talent acquisition, and product development. Dropbox also expanded its global presence, opening offices in various countries to cater to an increasingly diverse user base.

As Dropbox grew, it expanded beyond the consumer market and entered the enterprise space. The company introduced Dropbox for Business, targeting organizations and offering enhanced security, administrative controls, and collaboration features tailored to the needs of businesses.

In 2018, Dropbox went public with an initial public offering (IPO) on the NASDAQ stock exchange, solidifying its status as a leading player in the cloud storage and collaboration industry.

Over the years, Dropbox has continued to innovate and evolve its offerings. The company introduced advanced features such as file versioning, smart sync, and advanced sharing options. It has also ventured into new areas such as document collaboration and e-signature services to further empower users and businesses.

The story of Dropbox demonstrates the transformative impact of cloud storage technology on the way we store, access, and share information. From its humble beginnings as a startup, Dropbox has grown into a household name, empowering millions of individuals and businesses to work more efficiently and collaboratively.

Today, Dropbox remains committed to its mission of simplifying people's lives and revolutionizing the way we manage our digital content. Through continuous innovation and a focus on user experience, Dropbox continues to shape the future of cloud storage and collaboration, inspiring individuals and organizations to unleash their full potential.

15. Facebook

Founded in 2004 by Mark Zuckerberg, along with his college roommates Eduardo Saverin, Andrew McCollum, Dustin Moskovitz, and Chris Hughes, Facebook has redefined the way people connect, communicate, and share information globally.

Facebook originated as a social networking platform designed exclusively for Harvard University students. Named "Thefacebook," the website allowed students to create profiles, connect with classmates, and share updates and photos. The platform gained rapid popularity within the Harvard community, prompting Zuckerberg and his team to expand its reach to other Ivy League universities and gradually to universities across the United States.

As the user base grew exponentially, Facebook caught the attention of investors and venture capitalists, leading to crucial investments and the relocation of the company to California's Silicon Valley. Facebook's expansion continued, opening its doors to high school students and eventually becoming available to anyone aged 13 and above.

In 2006, Facebook underwent a significant transformation by introducing the News Feed feature. The News Feed became a central hub where users could see real-time updates from their friends, pages they followed, and other relevant content. Although initially met with some resistance, the News Feed became a defining feature of Facebook, enhancing user engagement and creating a more dynamic and interactive experience.

Facebook's global reach expanded beyond the United States, attracting users from around the world. The company introduced multilingual support, enabling users to access the platform in their native languages. This move facilitated Facebook's rapid international growth, establishing its presence as a leading global social media platform.

In 2008, Facebook launched the Facebook Platform, an initiative that allowed third-party developers to build applications within the Facebook ecosystem. This move led to a surge in the creation of games, quizzes, and other interactive experiences on the platform, enhancing user engagement and attracting more users.

One of Facebook's most significant milestones came in 2012 when the company went public with an initial public offering (IPO), valuing the company at billions of dollars. The IPO made Mark Zuckerberg one of the world's youngest billionaires and solidified Facebook's status as a dominant player in the tech industry.

Facebook continued to innovate and acquire other companies to expand its offerings. In 2012, the company acquired Instagram, a popular photo-sharing platform, and later in 2014, it acquired WhatsApp, a leading messaging app. These acquisitions not only expanded Facebook's user base but also added new dimensions to its services, positioning the company as a comprehensive social media and messaging powerhouse.

As Facebook grew, it faced numerous challenges related to user privacy, data security, and the spread of misinformation. The company has made efforts to address these issues by implementing stricter privacy controls, investing in content moderation, and partnering with fact-checking organizations to combat misinformation.

In recent years, Facebook has expanded its scope beyond social networking. The company has invested in virtual reality (VR) technology through its acquisition of Oculus VR, aiming to revolutionize the way people interact and experience digital content. Facebook has also ventured into cryptocurrency with the introduction of Libra, later renamed Diem, aiming to provide a global digital currency and financial infrastructure.

Today, Facebook boasts over 2.8 billion monthly active users worldwide, making it the largest social media platform in the world. The company continues to innovate, introducing new features such as Facebook Live, Marketplace, and Watch to enhance user engagement and diversify its offerings.

The story of Facebook represents the power of social connectivity and the impact of technological innovation. From its humble beginnings in a college dorm room, Facebook has grown into a global phenomenon, reshaping the way we communicate, share information, and build communities. With its continued focus on innovation and connecting people, Facebook remains at the forefront of the social media landscape, shaping the future of digital communication.

16. Fitbit

Fitbit was a pioneer in wearable technology, health tracking, and the pursuit of personal fitness goals. Founded in 2007 by James Park and Eric Friedman, Fitbit has played a significant role in the growth and popularity of the fitness tracker industry.

The inspiration for Fitbit came from James Park's personal struggle to lose weight and stay fit. He recognized the need for a device that could accurately track activity levels, monitor health metrics, and provide motivation for individuals striving to lead healthier lifestyles. With this vision, Park and Friedman set out to create a wearable device that would revolutionize the way people approached fitness and wellness.

Fitbit's first product, released in 2009, was a small activity tracker that users could wear on their wrists or clip onto clothing. The device used advanced sensors to measure steps taken, calories burned, distance traveled, and even sleep patterns. It provided users with real-time feedback, empowering them to make informed decisions about their health and activity levels.

Fitbit's commitment to accuracy, reliability, and user-friendly design quickly set it apart from competitors. The company continued to innovate and release new products, introducing features such as heart rate monitoring, GPS tracking, and advanced sleep tracking.

These enhancements allowed users to gain deeper insights into their overall health and wellness.

Fitbit's success was fueled by its comprehensive software platform. The company developed a user-friendly mobile app and web-based dashboard that synced seamlessly with the Fitbit devices. The app provided detailed data visualizations, goal tracking, and social features that allowed users to compete with friends and family, fostering a sense of community and motivation.

Fitbit's popularity grew rapidly, and the company became synonymous with fitness tracking. It expanded its product line to include a variety of trackers catering to different needs and preferences, ranging from basic models to more advanced ones with additional features and functionalities.

In 2015, Fitbit made its debut on the New York Stock Exchange with an initial public offering (IPO), becoming a publicly traded company. This milestone reflected the growing demand for wearable fitness technology and positioned Fitbit as a leading player in the industry.

Fitbit's success faced challenges with the emergence of smartwatches and the integration of fitness tracking features into these devices. To stay competitive, Fitbit expanded its product portfolio to include smartwatches with integrated fitness tracking capabilities, combining the best of both worlds. These smartwatches offered advanced features like smartphone notifications, music control, and contactless payments, while still prioritizing health and wellness tracking.

In 2020, Google announced its acquisition of Fitbit, signaling a new chapter for the company. With Google's resources and expertise in data analytics and software development, Fitbit aims to enhance its offerings and provide users with even more personalized health and wellness experiences.

Fitbit's impact extends beyond individual users. The company has collaborated with healthcare providers, insurers, and corporate wellness programs to promote healthier lifestyles and encourage physical activity. Fitbit's data insights and analytics have also contributed to valuable research studies on population health and fitness trends.

The story of Fitbit demonstrates the power of wearable technology in empowering individuals to take charge of their health and well-being. Fitbit's continuous innovation, accurate tracking, and user-friendly approach have made it a trusted companion for millions of people worldwide on their fitness journeys. With its acquisition by Google, Fitbit is poised to further revolutionize the health and wellness industry, leveraging cutting-edge technology to improve lives and inspire positive lifestyle changes.

17. Google

Google went from a small search engine to growing to one of the most influential technology companies in the world at incredible speed. Founded in 1998 by Larry Page and Sergey Brin, two Stanford University students, Google has revolutionized the way we access information, connect with others, and navigate the digital landscape.

The origins of Google can be traced back to a research project undertaken by Page and Brin while pursuing their Ph.D. studies. They developed a search engine algorithm called PageRank, which aimed to rank web pages based on their relevance and importance, considering factors such as links from other reputable sites. This breakthrough algorithm formed the foundation for the creation of Google.

In September 1998, Page and Brin officially launched Google as a search engine, initially operating out of a garage in Menlo Park, California. Google's minimalist design, fast and accurate search results, and emphasis on user experience set it apart from existing search engines at the time.

As word of Google's effectiveness spread, its user base grew rapidly, prompting the need for more robust infrastructure and additional talent. In 1999, the company secured its first major investment, and with the guidance of experienced executives like Eric

Schmidt, Google began to expand its operations and scale its technology.

Google's commitment to providing users with the most relevant and reliable search results led to continuous innovation and the introduction of new services. In 2000, Google launched Google AdWords, an advertising program that allowed businesses to display targeted ads alongside search results, revolutionizing the digital advertising landscape.

Recognizing the potential for growth beyond search, Google expanded its offerings by acquiring companies and developing new products. In 2004, the company launched Gmail, a free web-based email service that offered large storage capacity and innovative features. This move challenged established email providers and set a new standard for email communication.

In 2005, Google made a significant acquisition by purchasing Android Inc., a company focused on developing a mobile operating system. This acquisition laid the foundation for Google's entry into the smartphone market, culminating in the launch of the Android operating system in 2007. Today, Android is the most widely used mobile operating system globally.

Google's commitment to organizing and making information universally accessible extended beyond text-based content. The company launched Google Images, Google Maps, and Google News, among other services, expanding its reach into visual content, mapping, and news aggregation.

In 2004, Google made its initial public offering (IPO), and its shares began trading on the NASDAQ stock exchange. The IPO made Larry Page and Sergey Brin billionaires and provided the necessary resources for Google's continued expansion and acquisition of other companies.

Google's acquisitions have played a vital role in diversifying its offerings and expanding its technological capabilities. In 2006, the company acquired YouTube, the world's largest video-sharing platform, enabling Google to tap into the rapidly growing online video market. Subsequent acquisitions included companies like DoubleClick (digital advertising), Nest Labs (smart home technology), and DeepMind Technologies (artificial intelligence).

Google's commitment to innovation and pushing boundaries led to the development of groundbreaking products and services. In 2010, the company launched Google Translate, a machine translation service that enables users to translate text between different languages. Google also invested in autonomous vehicle technology through its subsidiary, Waymo, aiming to revolutionize transportation.

In 2015, Google underwent a corporate restructuring and formed Alphabet Inc., a conglomerate that encompasses Google and other subsidiary companies. This move allowed Google to focus on its core search and advertising businesses while promoting the growth of other ventures under the Alphabet umbrella.

Today, Google is much more than a search engine. It has become a technology powerhouse, offering a wide range of products and services, including cloud computing, productivity

tools, smart home devices, and more. Google's influence extends to artificial intelligence, machine learning, and data analytics, driving advancements in various industries and shaping the future of technology.

Throughout its journey, Google has remained committed to its founding principles, including a focus on user experience, organizing the world's information, and making it universally accessible. With its mission to "organize the world's information and make it universally accessible and useful," Google continues to push the boundaries of technology and shape the digital landscape we live in.

18. GoPro

Founded in 2002 by Nick Woodman, GoPro has revolutionized the way people document and share their adventures. The inspiration for GoPro came during a surfing trip that Nick Woodman took to Australia. Frustrated by the limitations of existing cameras in capturing high-quality action shots, Woodman saw an opportunity to develop a versatile camera that could withstand extreme conditions and provide immersive footage.

Woodman started working on his vision and, with a small budget, began building a durable and portable camera. He used his own experience as an avid surfer and adventurer to design a camera that could be worn or mounted on various equipment, allowing users to capture unique and immersive perspectives.

In 2004, GoPro introduced its first camera, the GoPro HERO. This small, waterproof, and shockproof camera quickly gained popularity among action sports enthusiasts, who were captivated by the ability to record their adventures hands-free and share the footage with others.

GoPro's success was driven by its commitment to providing high-quality and easy-to-use cameras. The company continued to innovate and release new camera models with enhanced features and capabilities, such as improved image quality, higher frame rates, and built-in Wi-Fi connectivity for seamless content sharing.

GoPro's innovative marketing strategies also played a significant role in its growth. The company leveraged user-generated content by encouraging users to share their GoPro footage, creating a community of passionate users who became brand ambassadors. This strategy, combined with captivating marketing campaigns and partnerships with professional athletes, helped GoPro gain widespread recognition and establish itself as a leading action camera brand.

GoPro's success expanded beyond the action sports market. Its cameras found applications in various industries, including filmmaking, journalism, travel, and even professional videography. The company continuously improved its product lineup, introducing advanced features like image stabilization, voice control, and live streaming capabilities.

However, GoPro faced challenges as the action camera market became more competitive, with new entrants offering similar products at lower prices. In addition, the company experienced setbacks with product recalls and manufacturing issues. These factors led to declining sales and financial difficulties for GoPro.

To adapt to changing market dynamics, GoPro shifted its focus from solely manufacturing cameras to providing a broader ecosystem of products and services. The company launched the GoPro Plus subscription service, offering cloud storage, camera replacement, and other benefits to subscribers. It also introduced the GoPro Karma drone, expanding its product portfolio into aerial photography and videography.

Despite the challenges, GoPro has persevered and regained momentum through strategic product improvements and cost-cutting measures. The company has continued to release new camera models, such as the HERO8 and HERO9, incorporating advanced features and refinements based on user feedback.

GoPro's impact extends beyond hardware. The company

developed the Quik mobile app and GoPro Studio software, enabling users to easily edit and share their footage. These tools provide intuitive editing capabilities, allowing users to create professional-quality videos with minimal effort.

Today, GoPro remains a trusted name in the action camera market, synonymous with capturing and sharing adventures. The company's commitment to innovation, durability, and immersive content creation has solidified its position as a leader in the industry.

The story of GoPro exemplifies the power of entrepreneurial spirit and the ability to turn a passion into a successful business. From humble beginnings, GoPro has transformed the way we document and experience our adventures, empowering individuals to capture breathtaking moments and share them with the world.

19. IBM

The story of IBM (International Business Machines Corporation) is a journey through the evolution of technology and the emergence of a global technology giant. Established in 1911 as the Computing-Tabulating-Recording Company (CTR), IBM has played a pivotal role in shaping the modern computing industry.

IBM's early years were marked by innovation in data processing and tabulation equipment. It initially focused on developing and selling time clocks, scales, and tabulating machines, which were widely used by businesses for data processing and record-keeping. Under the leadership of Thomas J. Watson Sr., the company expanded its operations and quickly became a dominant player in the industry.

In 1924, the company changed its name to International Business Machines Corporation (IBM), reflecting its broader global aspirations. Throughout the 1930s and 1940s, IBM continued to innovate and develop advanced tabulating machines, including the famous IBM 405, which became a standard tool for processing census data.

IBM's story took a significant turn during World War II when it played a crucial role in supporting the war effort. The company worked closely with the United States government, providing critical technology and support for various military projects, including the development of advanced calculating machines and code-breaking systems.

Following the war, IBM capitalized on its expertise in data processing and computing technology to expand into the emerging field of electronic computers. In 1952, the company introduced the IBM 701, its first commercially successful computer. This marked the beginning of IBM's transformation into a leader in the computer industry.

IBM's commitment to research and development led to numerous breakthroughs in computer technology. In the 1960s, the company introduced the IBM System/360, a family of compatible computers that set a new industry standard for compatibility and scalability. This landmark achievement positioned IBM as a leading provider of mainframe computers, which were essential for large-scale data processing and business applications.

Throughout the following decades, IBM continued to innovate and introduce new technologies and products. It played a vital role in the development of magnetic storage devices, such as the hard disk drive, and pioneered the creation of advanced computer programming languages and software.

IBM's influence extended beyond hardware and software. It became a trusted partner for businesses worldwide, offering a range of services, including consulting, system integration, and outsourcing. IBM's expertise and extensive client base allowed it to provide comprehensive solutions tailored to the needs of various industries and sectors.

In the 1980s and 1990s, IBM faced significant challenges as the computing industry underwent rapid changes. The rise of personal computers and the emergence of competitors posed threats to IBM's market dominance. However, under the leadership of executives like Lou Gerstner, IBM undertook a strategic transformation, focusing on providing comprehensive solutions and embracing emerging technologies.

IBM expanded its portfolio to include services and software, aiming to deliver integrated solutions that combined hardware, software, and services to address complex business challenges. The company's commitment to innovation led to groundbreaking developments, such as the creation of the relational database management system (DB2) and the introduction of the IBM Watson AI platform.

Today, IBM is a global technology and consulting powerhouse, serving clients in various industries and sectors. It has diversified its offerings, including cloud computing services, artificial intelligence, blockchain technology, and cybersecurity solutions. IBM's dedication to research and development remains a driving force behind its success, with its renowned IBM Research division making significant contributions to scientific and technological advancements.

IBM's impact extends beyond technology. The company has been a pioneer in corporate social responsibility, focusing on environmental sustainability, diversity and inclusion, and community engagement. It has consistently ranked among the world's most admired companies and has received recognition for its commitment to ethical business practices.

The story of IBM is a testament to the power of innovation, adaptability, and long-term vision

. From its humble beginnings as a tabulating machine manufacturer, IBM has evolved into a global technology leader, shaping the digital age and making a profound impact on businesses and society as a whole.

20. Impossible Foods

Impossible Foods is an inspiring journey of scientific innovation, environmental consciousness, and a mission to transform the global food system. Founded in 2011 by Dr. Patrick O. Brown, a renowned biochemist and entrepreneur, Impossible Foods has revolutionized the way we think about plant-based alternatives to meat.

Dr. Brown's motivation behind starting Impossible Foods stemmed from his deep concern about the detrimental environmental impact of animal agriculture. He recognized that finding a sustainable and scalable alternative to traditional meat consumption was crucial for the health of the planet. With a background in genetics, medicine, and biochemistry, Dr. Brown set out to tackle this challenge head-on.

The breakthrough innovation at the heart of Impossible Foods is the creation of the Impossible Burger. Unlike conventional veggie burgers, which often fail to deliver the taste and texture of real meat, the Impossible Burger is designed to replicate the sensory experience of eating meat while being entirely plant-based.

The key ingredient that sets the Impossible Burger apart is heme, a molecule found in both plants and animals that contributes to the unique taste and aroma of meat. Dr. Brown and his team discovered a way to extract heme from plants, specifically from soybean roots, and produce it at scale using fermentation. This plant-based heme became the core element in creating the meaty flavor of the Impossible Burger.

The development of the Impossible Burger involved extensive scientific research, rigorous testing, and collaboration with a team of scientists, chefs, and food experts. The goal was to create a product that not only satisfied the taste buds of meat lovers but also had a significantly smaller environmental footprint compared to traditional beef.

In 2016, Impossible Foods unveiled the first version of the Impossible Burger, initially launching it in select restaurants and food establishments. The burger gained attention for its striking resemblance to real meat, its juiciness, and the fact that it even "bled" like a traditional burger, thanks to the heme.

As awareness of the environmental impact of animal agriculture grew, so did the demand for sustainable alternatives. Impossible Foods rapidly expanded its production capabilities and partnerships with various restaurants and foodservice providers, making the Impossible Burger more widely available to consumers across the United States and beyond.

The company's commitment to innovation and continuous improvement led to the launch of the next-generation Impossible Burger, known as the Impossible Burger 2.0, in 2019. This improved version boasted an even more realistic taste, texture, and versatility, making it a preferred choice for both meat-eaters and vegetarians alike.

Impossible Foods' impact has extended beyond the creation of the Impossible Burger. The company's focus on sustainability has resonated with consumers, leading to increased interest in plant-based alternatives and prompting conversations about the future of food. The success of Impossible Foods has also spurred competitors and encouraged other food companies to explore plant-based innovations.

In addition to its environmental goals, Impossible Foods aims to address global food security by reducing reliance on animal agriculture and its associated resource-intensive practices. By developing plant-based alternatives that are indistinguishable from traditional meat products, the company seeks to provide a scalable and sustainable solution to feeding a growing global population.

Today, Impossible Foods continues to innovate and expand its product lineup, introducing new plant-based offerings beyond the burger, such as ground meat and sausage. The company's products can be found in numerous restaurants, fast-food chains, and grocery stores, catering to the growing demand for sustainable and delicious plant-based options.

The story of Impossible Foods showcases the power of science, technology, and entrepreneurship in tackling pressing environmental challenges. By combining scientific expertise with culinary creativity, Impossible Foods has paved the way for a new era of plant-based food innovation, redefining what is possible in creating a sustainable and appetizing future for our food system.

21. Incyte

Incyte Corporation is a biopharmaceutical company that has made significant contributions to the field of drug discovery and development. Founded in 1991 by Roy Whitfield, Incyte set out to leverage genomic research to unlock the secrets of the human genome and develop innovative therapies for serious diseases.

The story of Incyte begins with its focus on genomics, a field that was gaining momentum in the early 1990s. Whitfield believed that understanding the human genome could provide valuable insights into disease mechanisms and pave the way for the development of targeted treatments.

Incyte's first breakthrough came in 1992 when the company successfully isolated the first full-length gene, known as the epidermal growth factor receptor (EGFR). This achievement laid the foundation for Incyte's subsequent advancements in genomics research.

By building a robust genomic database, Incyte developed tools and technologies to analyze and interpret the vast amount of genomic data being generated. The company's efforts resulted in the creation of the LifeSeq Gene Index, one of the most comprehensive genomic databases at the time. This database became a valuable resource for scientists and researchers worldwide, facilitating the discovery of new genes and potential drug targets.

As Incyte continued to expand its capabilities, it shifted its focus towards drug discovery and development. Leveraging its genomic expertise, the company embarked on identifying and validating potential drug targets for various diseases, including cancer, inflammation, and autoimmune disorders.

One of Incyte's pivotal achievements came in 2011 with the approval of its first drug, ruxolitinib, under the brand name Jakafi®. Jakafi, an oral medication, was the first JAK inhibitor approved by the U.S. Food and Drug Administration (FDA) for the treatment of myelofibrosis, a rare blood cancer. This breakthrough marked a significant milestone for Incyte, as it demonstrated the company's ability to translate genomic research into effective therapies.

Since the approval of Jakafi, Incyte has continued to make strides in developing innovative treatments for various diseases. The company's pipeline includes investigational drugs targeting hematologic malignancies, solid tumors, and inflammatory disorders.

In addition to its drug development efforts, Incyte has forged strategic partnerships and collaborations with other pharmaceutical companies, academic institutions, and research organizations. These collaborations have further enhanced Incyte's capabilities in genomics research, drug discovery, and clinical development.

Today, Incyte is recognized as a leading biopharmaceutical company with a strong commitment to scientific innovation and patient-centered care. Its contributions to precision medicine and the development of targeted therapies have had a profound impact on the lives of patients around the world.

The story of Incyte is a testament to the power of genomics and its potential to transform healthcare. Through its dedication to scientific excellence, rigorous research, and collaboration, Incyte continues to advance the understanding of diseases and develop groundbreaking treatments that address unmet medical needs.

As Incyte strives to improve patient outcomes and shape the future of medicine, its story serves as an inspiration to the biopharmaceutical industry, researchers, and healthcare professionals alike.

22. Intel

Intel is a tale of innovation, leadership, and the relentless pursuit of advancements in the field of semiconductors. Established in 1968 by Robert Noyce and Gordon Moore, Intel has become one of the most influential and dominant players in the global semiconductor industry.

Intel's origins can be traced back to the early days of the semiconductor revolution. Robert Noyce and Gordon Moore, both talented engineers who had previously worked at Fairchild Semiconductor, saw an opportunity to create a new company that could leverage their expertise in integrated circuits.

In its early years, Intel focused on developing memory chips, specifically static random-access memory (SRAM) chips. The company's first commercially successful product, the 3101 Schottky bipolar random-access memory (RAM), helped establish Intel as a reliable and innovative semiconductor manufacturer.

However, Intel's true breakthrough came in 1971 when it introduced the world's first commercially available microprocessor, the Intel 4004. Developed by a team led by Ted Hoff, the Intel 4004 was a revolutionary invention that integrated the functions of multiple electronic components onto a single chip. This breakthrough led to the birth of the microprocessor industry and laid the foundation for the digital revolution.

Over the years, Intel continued to push the boundaries of semiconductor technology and played a crucial role in the development of the personal computer (PC) industry. The company's microprocessors, such as the Intel 8080 and the Intel 8086, became the standard processors for early PCs, powering the growth and popularity of these machines.

Intel's commitment to innovation and its ability to deliver increasingly powerful and efficient microprocessors solidified its position as a leader in the industry. The company's "Tick-Tock" strategy, introduced in 2006, alternated between introducing a new microarchitecture ("tick") and a new manufacturing process ("tock") with each product generation, ensuring consistent performance improvements and technological advancements.

Intel's processors became the backbone of the PC industry, powering millions of computers worldwide. The company's reputation for performance and reliability made the "Intel Inside" logo a trusted symbol of quality and technological excellence.

In addition to its success in the PC market, Intel expanded its product portfolio to include a wide range of semiconductor solutions, including chipsets, memory modules, network interface controllers, and solid-state drives. The company's technology found applications in various industries, from telecommunications to healthcare, automotive, and beyond.

However, Intel faced increasing competition as the semiconductor industry evolved. Rival companies, such as AMD, emerged with competitive offerings, challenging Intel's dominance. The rise of mobile devices and the shift towards low-power processors also posed new challenges for Intel.

To adapt to these market changes, Intel diversified its focus and made strategic acquisitions to expand its capabilities. The company acquired Altera Corporation in 2015, strengthening its position in the field of field-programmable gate arrays (FPGAs) and customizable semiconductor solutions.

Intel also ventured into new areas of technology, including artificial intelligence (AI), autonomous vehicles, and the Internet of Things (IoT). The company's commitment to advancing technology and its strong research and development capabilities enabled it to explore new frontiers and seize opportunities in emerging markets.

Today, Intel continues to innovate and deliver cutting-edge semiconductor solutions. The company's processors power a wide range of devices, from PCs and servers to data centers and cloud computing infrastructure. Intel's influence extends to areas like AI, high-performance computing, and autonomous systems, where its technologies are driving transformative advancements.

The story of Intel is not just about the creation of powerful microprocessors; it is a testament to the power of innovation, engineering prowess, and strategic vision. From revolutionizing the semiconductor industry with the microprocessor to embracing new frontiers of technology, Intel has shaped the digital age and left an indelible mark on the world of computing and beyond.

23. Lyft

Founded in 2012 by Logan Green and John Zimmer, Lyft has grown from a small startup with a vision into a global leader in the ride-hailing market. The idea behind Lyft was born out of the founders' desire to tackle the challenges of traffic congestion, limited parking, and the high costs associated with owning a car. They envisioned a platform that would connect people who needed rides with available drivers, making transportation more accessible, affordable, and efficient.

Lyft launched its service in San Francisco in June 2012, initially operating as a peer-to-peer ride-sharing platform, connecting passengers with drivers who used their personal vehicles. The company differentiated itself from traditional taxi services by embracing a more community-oriented and friendly approach, encouraging passengers to sit in the front seat and fostering a sense of camaraderie.

To establish trust and safety within the platform, Lyft implemented a robust rating system, allowing passengers and drivers to rate each other after each ride. This feedback mechanism played a vital role in maintaining a high level of service quality and building a reliable and trustworthy ride-sharing network.

As Lyft gained popularity and expanded its operations to more cities across the United States, the company introduced various service options to cater to different customer needs. In 2013, Lyft launched Lyft Line, a carpooling service that allowed passengers heading in the same direction to share a ride and split the cost. This innovative approach aimed to reduce congestion and make rides more affordable for passengers.

Lyft's growth was driven by its ability to create a seamless user experience through its mobile app. Passengers could request rides with just a few taps on their smartphones, track the arrival of their driver in real-time, and make cashless transactions through the app. The company also prioritized driver satisfaction, offering flexible work arrangements and incentives to attract and retain drivers.

In 2017, Lyft expanded its presence internationally by launching its service in Toronto, Canada, marking its first venture outside of the United States. This move signaled Lyft's ambition to become a global player in the ride-sharing industry.

To stay competitive and diversify its offerings, Lyft ventured into other transportation sectors. In 2019, the company launched Lyft Bikes and Scooters, providing dockless electric bikes and scooters as an alternative mode of urban transportation. This expansion into micro-mobility showcased Lyft's commitment to sustainable and multimodal transportation solutions.

Lyft's journey has not been without challenges. The company faced regulatory hurdles, opposition from taxi associations, and competition from other ride-sharing platforms. However, its focus on safety, reliability, and a commitment to building strong relationships with drivers and passengers helped Lyft overcome these obstacles and cement its position in the market.

Lyft went public in March 2019, listing its shares on the Nasdaq stock exchange. This marked a significant milestone for the company, reflecting its growth and market value. The public offering provided Lyft with additional capital to invest in technology development, expand its services, and explore new opportunities.

Today, Lyft operates in hundreds of cities across the United States and Canada, serving millions of riders and connecting them with a network of drivers. The company continues to innovate and explore new avenues, including autonomous vehicle technology and partnerships with public transportation agencies to integrate ride-sharing with existing transit systems.

The story of Lyft showcases the transformative power of technology in revolutionizing traditional industries. By embracing the sharing economy model and leveraging mobile technology, Lyft has reimagined the way people commute, reducing the reliance on personal car ownership and offering more sustainable and efficient transportation options.

24. Microsoft

Founded by Bill Gates and Paul Allen in 1975, Microsoft has become one of the most influential and iconic companies in the history of the computer industry. The journey of Microsoft began in Albuquerque, New Mexico, where Bill Gates and Paul Allen seized the opportunity to develop software for the Altair 8800, one of the first personal computers. They created a programming language called Altair BASIC, which quickly gained popularity among computer enthusiasts and established Microsoft as a provider of software solutions.

In 1981, Microsoft took a major leap forward with the launch of MS-DOS (Microsoft Disk Operating System), a simple yet powerful operating system for IBM-compatible personal computers. MS-DOS became the de facto standard for PC operating systems, providing a stable foundation for software development and establishing Microsoft as a key player in the emerging PC industry.

The breakthrough moment for Microsoft came with the release of Windows in 1985. Windows was a graphical user interface (GUI) that introduced a more intuitive and user-friendly way of interacting with computers. It brought elements such as icons, windows, and a mouse-driven cursor to the PC, making computing accessible to a broader audience. Windows quickly gained widespread adoption and set the stage for Microsoft's dominance in the operating system market.

As Microsoft continued to expand its product portfolio, it ventured into other software categories, including office productivity tools. The introduction of Microsoft Office in 1989, which included applications like Word, Excel, and PowerPoint, revolutionized the way people worked, providing them with powerful tools to create, analyze, and present information.

Throughout the 1990s and early 2000s, Microsoft solidified its position as the leading software company, fueled by a series of successful product releases and strategic acquisitions. The Windows operating system continued to evolve, with releases like Windows 95, Windows XP, and Windows 7, introducing new features and improvements to enhance user experience.

In 2001, Microsoft entered the gaming console market with the launch of the Xbox, a video game console that brought immersive gaming experiences to millions of players worldwide. The subsequent releases of Xbox 360 and Xbox One further cemented Microsoft's presence in the gaming industry and positioned it as a major competitor to established players like Sony and Nintendo.

Microsoft's commitment to innovation led to the development of other groundbreaking technologies. The company invested heavily in research and development, leading to advancements in areas such as artificial intelligence, cloud computing, and productivity tools. Products and services like Azure, Microsoft 365, and Teams have transformed the way businesses operate and collaborate, fueling Microsoft's growth and expanding its reach into enterprise markets.

In recent years, Microsoft has embraced a cloud-first strategy, focusing on its Azure cloud platform and services. Azure has emerged as a leading cloud computing platform, enabling organizations to build, deploy, and manage applications and services on a global scale.

Under the leadership of Satya Nadella, who became CEO in 2014, Microsoft underwent a cultural shift, embracing openness, collaboration, and a growth mindset. This shift propelled Microsoft's success in the cloud market, fostering partnerships with other tech giants and positioning the company as a leader in the digital transformation era.

Today, Microsoft continues to innovate across various domains, ranging from software development and cloud computing to gaming, artificial intelligence, and beyond. Its products and services touch the lives of billions of people worldwide, empowering individuals, businesses, and organizations to achieve more.

The story of Microsoft exemplifies the power of entrepreneurial vision, technological innovation, and strategic adaptability. Through its relentless pursuit of software excellence, Microsoft has left an indelible mark on the technology industry and continues to shape the future of computing.

25. Moderna

The story of Moderna is a remarkable tale of scientific breakthroughs, innovation, and a relentless commitment to advancing the field of mRNA (messenger RNA) technology. Founded in 2010 by a group of entrepreneurs and scientists, Moderna has emerged as a leader in the development of mRNA-based vaccines and therapies.

Moderna's journey began with the vision to harness the power of mRNA to revolutionize medicine. mRNA is a molecule that carries instructions for protein synthesis in cells, and Moderna saw its potential to create a new class of medicines that could address unmet medical needs.

The company's early years were focused on extensive research and development efforts to refine the understanding and application of mRNA technology. Moderna built a strong foundation of scientific knowledge and expertise, paving the way for groundbreaking discoveries and advancements.

In 2012, Moderna made headlines by demonstrating the successful delivery of mRNA-based drugs into living organisms. This achievement marked a significant milestone in the development of mRNA therapeutics, showcasing the potential of this technology to treat various diseases and conditions.

One of Moderna's most significant breakthroughs came in 2020 when the company developed and received emergency use authorization for its mRNA-based COVID-19 vaccine, known as the Moderna COVID-19 vaccine or mRNA-1273. The development of the vaccine was a result of Moderna's collaboration with the National Institute of Allergy and Infectious Diseases (NIAID) and the Biomedical Advanced Research and Development Authority (BARDA).

The Moderna COVID-19 vaccine demonstrated high efficacy in clinical trials, offering hope and contributing to global efforts to combat the COVID-19 pandemic. The success of the vaccine propelled Moderna to the forefront of the biotechnology industry, solidifying its position as a leader in mRNA technology.

Beyond the COVID-19 vaccine, Moderna continues to innovate and develop mRNA-based therapeutics for various diseases. The versatility of mRNA technology allows for the creation of personalized medicines tailored to specific genetic profiles and medical conditions.

Moderna's mRNA platform has the potential to revolutionize the treatment of infectious diseases, cancer, genetic disorders, and other conditions that have traditionally posed significant challenges in drug development. The company's pipeline includes mRNA-based vaccines and therapies targeting a range of diseases, providing new hope for patients and medical professionals alike.

The success of Moderna is attributed not only to its scientific advancements but also to its collaborative approach and strategic partnerships. The company has formed collaborations with academic institutions, government agencies, and pharmaceutical companies to leverage expertise, resources, and infrastructure, accelerating the development and commercialization of mRNA-based therapies.

Moderna's achievements have not only transformed the landscape of medicine but have also had a profound impact on the biotechnology industry as a whole. The company's groundbreaking mRNA technology has sparked a new wave of research and development, inspiring other companies and researchers to explore the potential of mRNA-based therapeutics.

The story of Moderna is a testament to the power of innovation, resilience, and a relentless pursuit of scientific excellence. Through its pioneering work in mRNA technology, Moderna has redefined what is possible in the field of medicine, offering new hope for patients and potentially revolutionizing the way diseases are treated and prevented.

26. Naver

Naver is a South Korean technology company that has become a household name and a dominant force in the country's digital landscape. Founded in 1999 by Lee Hae-jin, Naver began as a search engine striving to provide Korean internet users with a localized and comprehensive search experience.

In the early days, Naver faced stiff competition from global search giants like Google and Yahoo, but it quickly differentiated itself by focusing on the specific needs and preferences of the Korean audience. Naver understood that language nuances, cultural context, and local content were essential to capturing the attention of Korean internet users.

One of Naver's early breakthroughs came with the introduction of its innovative search algorithm called "Knowledge iN." This algorithm enabled Naver to deliver more accurate and relevant search results, incorporating contextual information from blogs, forums, and other online communities. Naver's search engine rapidly gained popularity among Korean users, cementing its position as the go-to search platform in the country.

Recognizing the potential of expanding beyond search, Naver continued to evolve and diversify its offerings. In 2002, the company launched its webcomic platform, Naver Webtoon, which quickly became a sensation. Naver Webtoon revolutionized the way comics were consumed by introducing a digital, mobile-friendly format with regular updates, interactive features, and a vast library of diverse genres. It became a cultural phenomenon, attracting millions of readers and spawning a new generation of webcomic artists.

Naver's success did not stop there. In 2003, the company introduced Naver Café, an online community platform that allowed users to create and join interest-based communities. Naver Café provided a space for individuals to connect, share information, and engage in discussions, fostering a vibrant online community culture.

As Naver continued to expand its services, it made strategic acquisitions to enhance its capabilities. In 2004, Naver acquired Hangame, a leading online gaming company, which allowed it to venture into the lucrative gaming industry. This move helped Naver solidify its position as a comprehensive online platform offering search, webcomics, community, and gaming services.

In subsequent years, Naver launched a range of innovative services, including Naver Blog, Naver Knowledge iN, and Naver Music. The company also made significant advancements in artificial intelligence (AI) technology, developing its virtual assistant called Naver Clova and investing in research and development in areas such as autonomous vehicles and robotics.

Today, Naver has evolved into a conglomerate known as Naver Corporation, offering a wide array of digital services and platforms. It operates in various sectors, including search, e-commerce, fintech, entertainment, and more. Naver's influence extends beyond South Korea, with its services and technologies making an impact globally.

Naver's success story is a testament to its relentless focus on understanding and meeting the specific needs of its users. By tailoring its services to the Korean audience and continually innovating to provide engaging and valuable experiences, Naver has become an integral part of the country's digital ecosystem.

As Naver continues to expand its horizons and push the

boundaries of technology, its story serves as an inspiration to entrepreneurs and companies worldwide. It highlights the importance of localizing products and services, anticipating user needs, and constantly innovating to stay ahead in a rapidly evolving digital landscape.

27. Netflix

From its humble beginnings as a DVD-by-mail service to its current status as a global streaming giant, Netflix has revolutionized the way people consume movies and television shows. Netflix was founded in 1997 by Reed Hastings and Marc Randolph, with the initial goal of creating a more convenient and efficient way for people to rent movies. The company introduced a subscription-based model that allowed customers to rent DVDs online and have them delivered by mail. This eliminated the need for physical video rental stores and late fees, providing a convenient alternative for movie enthusiasts.

In its early years, Netflix faced challenges and competition from established players in the industry. However, the company's focus on customer satisfaction and technological innovation set it apart. Netflix introduced a personalized recommendation algorithm that analyzed user preferences and viewing history to suggest movies and TV shows tailored to each individual's tastes. This personalized recommendation system became one of Netflix's key competitive advantages.

In 2007, Netflix took a significant leap forward with the introduction of its streaming service. This marked a pivotal moment in the company's history, as it shifted from a primarily DVD rental business to a streaming platform that allowed customers to watch content instantly over the internet. The streaming service initially offered a limited selection of movies and TV shows, but it laid the foundation for Netflix's future success.

To differentiate itself from traditional television networks and cable providers, Netflix began producing original content. The company's first foray into original programming came with the release of the series "House of Cards" in 2013, followed by other critically acclaimed shows like "Stranger Things," "Narcos," and "The Crown." These original productions showcased Netflix's commitment to high-quality storytelling and further solidified its position as a major player in the entertainment industry.

As streaming technology and internet infrastructure improved, Netflix expanded its reach globally. The company launched its streaming service internationally, allowing subscribers around the world to access its vast library of movies and TV shows. This global expansion propelled Netflix's growth and transformed it into a household name in the entertainment industry.

Netflix's success disrupted traditional media and entertainment models. The company's on-demand streaming platform and commitment to producing original content challenged the dominance of cable television and forced established networks to adapt to changing consumer preferences. Netflix pioneered the concept of binge-watching, where viewers could consume entire seasons of shows at their own pace, further changing the way people consumed entertainment.

In recent years, Netflix has faced increased competition from other streaming services, including industry giants like Amazon Prime Video and Disney+. However, the company continues to invest in content creation, technological innovation, and international expansion to stay ahead of the curve. It has expanded its content library to include a wide range of genres, catering to diverse audience preferences.

Today, Netflix boasts millions of subscribers worldwide and has become a cultural phenomenon. It continues to push the boundaries of storytelling, invest in original content, and leverage data analytics to provide a personalized and engaging entertainment experience for its subscribers.

The story of Netflix is a testament to the power of disruption, innovation, and adaptability. By embracing streaming technology, investing in original content, and staying attuned to changing consumer preferences, Netflix has redefined the entertainment landscape and shaped the way people around the world consume movies and TV shows.

28. NVIDIA

The history of NVIDIA is a fascinating journey that exemplifies the revolutionary potential of graphics processing technology as well as the firm's unwavering commitment to innovation. Founded in 1993 by Jensen Huang, Chris Malachowsky, and Curtis Priem, NVIDIA has become a global leader in visual computing and artificial intelligence.

NVIDIA initially focused on creating graphics processing units (GPUs) for the gaming industry. Its first product, the NV1, was released in 1995 and introduced revolutionary 3D graphics capabilities for PCs. This marked the beginning of NVIDIA's commitment to delivering high-performance GPUs that could handle complex graphics rendering and deliver immersive gaming experiences.

The breakthrough moment for NVIDIA came in 1999 with the release of the GeForce 256, a GPU that introduced hardware transform and lighting, a technique that offloaded computationally intensive tasks from the CPU to the GPU. This innovation paved the way for realistic and visually stunning graphics in games and established NVIDIA as a leading provider of graphics technology.

NVIDIA's focus expanded beyond gaming as it recognized the potential of GPUs in other industries. The company started collaborating with researchers and scientists, harnessing the parallel processing power of GPUs to accelerate scientific computations and data analysis. This led to the emergence of GPU computing and the development of CUDA (Compute Unified Device Architecture), a parallel computing platform and programming model that allows developers to utilize the power of GPUs for general-purpose computing.

In recent years, NVIDIA has made significant strides in artificial intelligence (AI) and deep learning. Its GPUs are uniquely suited for training and inference tasks in AI applications, enabling breakthroughs in areas such as autonomous vehicles, healthcare, and robotics. NVIDIA's advancements in AI technology have positioned the company at the forefront of the AI revolution, providing the computational power necessary to tackle complex problems and drive innovation across industries.

Furthermore, NVIDIA has expanded its portfolio beyond GPUs to include system-on-a-chip (SoC) solutions for mobile devices, autonomous driving platforms, and data center solutions. Its acquisition of ARM Holdings in 2020 further strengthens its position in the semiconductor industry and opens up new opportunities for growth and innovation.

NVIDIA's commitment to innovation and its relentless pursuit of pushing the boundaries of what is possible in visual computing and AI have earned it widespread recognition and numerous accolades. The company has received awards for its technology advancements, including multiple prestigious Turing Awards, often referred to as the Nobel Prize of computing.

Beyond technology, NVIDIA has also prioritized environmental sustainability. It has made significant efforts to reduce its carbon footprint, optimize energy efficiency, and support initiatives focused on environmental conservation and renewable energy.

Today, NVIDIA continues to drive innovation and shape the future of computing. Its GPUs power gaming experiences, enable scientific breakthroughs, and accelerate AI research. With a focus on cutting-edge technologies like ray tracing, real-time rendering, and deep learning, NVIDIA remains at the forefront of visual computing, delivering solutions that empower industries and transform the way we interact with technology.

The story of NVIDIA is a testament to the transformative power of graphics processing and the company's unwavering commitment to pushing the boundaries of what is possible. Through its innovative products, strategic partnerships, and dedication to technological advancement, NVIDIA has solidified its position as a leader in the semiconductor industry, leaving a lasting impact on the world of computing and beyond.

29. Palantir Technologies

Palantir Technologies' story is a gripping account of data-driven innovation, sophisticated analytics, and the use of technology to address challenging issues. Founded in 2003 by a group of entrepreneurs, including Peter Thiel, Alex Karp, and Joe Lonsdale, Palantir has emerged as a prominent player in the field of data integration and analysis.

The inspiration for Palantir came from the founders' recognition of the immense challenges faced by organizations in making sense of vast amounts of data and extracting meaningful insights. The company set out to develop a platform that could integrate and analyze disparate data sources, enabling organizations to gain valuable intelligence and make better-informed decisions.

Palantir's early years were characterized by intensive research and development efforts to build a robust software platform capable of handling complex data analysis tasks. The company pioneered the concept of data fusion, which involves integrating diverse datasets to create a comprehensive and cohesive view of information. This approach allows organizations to uncover hidden patterns, detect anomalies, and generate actionable insights.

One of Palantir's key products is its flagship software platform, Palantir Gotham (formerly known as Palantir Government). Gotham is designed to meet the needs of government agencies, intelligence organizations, and law enforcement entities, enabling them to collect, analyze, and visualize data from various sources in real-time. The platform has been instrumental in supporting critical missions related to national security, counterterrorism, and law enforcement.

In addition to Palantir Gotham, the company also developed Palantir Foundry, a platform designed for enterprise customers in industries such as finance, healthcare, and manufacturing. Foundry provides organizations with the tools and capabilities to integrate, transform, and analyze complex data, empowering them to make data-driven decisions and drive operational efficiencies.

Palantir's approach to data analysis is unique in that it combines advanced analytics with human intuition. The software platforms developed by Palantir are designed to augment human decision-making, providing analysts and investigators with powerful tools and visualizations to explore data and uncover meaningful insights. This human-centered approach sets Palantir apart from many other data analytics companies.

Over the years, Palantir has established itself as a trusted partner for governments, intelligence agencies, and enterprises around the world. Its solutions have been deployed in various high-profile projects, including counterterrorism efforts, disaster response, and fraud detection.

In 2020, Palantir made its debut as a publicly traded company, listing its shares on the New York Stock Exchange. The IPO marked a significant milestone in the company's journey and positioned Palantir for further growth and expansion.

Palantir's success has not come without controversy. The company has faced scrutiny over data privacy concerns and its involvement in controversial government programs. However, it remains committed to working transparently and ethically, ensuring that its technologies are used responsibly and in compliance with legal and regulatory frameworks.

The story of Palantir Technologies reflects the power of data analytics and the impact it can have on decision-making and problem-solving. By developing innovative software platforms and leveraging advanced analytics techniques, Palantir has transformed the way organizations approach data analysis, empowering them to derive actionable insights from complex and diverse datasets. As the field of data analytics continues to evolve, Palantir remains at the forefront, driving innovation and shaping the future of data-driven decision-making.

30. Patagonia

The story of Patagonia is a remarkable tale of a company driven by a deep commitment to environmental sustainability, ethical business practices, and a love for the outdoors. Founded in 1973 by Yvon Chouinard, Patagonia has become a global leader in the outdoor apparel and gear industry while advocating for environmental and social responsibility.

The journey of Patagonia began with Chouinard's passion for climbing and his desire to create high-quality climbing equipment. Initially named Chouinard Equipment, the company focused on designing and manufacturing innovative climbing gear using durable and sustainable materials. Chouinard's commitment to quality and craftsmanship quickly earned the company a reputation for excellence within the climbing community.

In the 1980s, Chouinard Equipment faced a turning point. Concerned about the environmental impact of his company's products, Chouinard realized the need for a shift towards more sustainable practices. The company made a bold decision to transition from using traditional materials like pitons (metal spikes used for climbing) to advocating for clean climbing techniques that minimized damage to natural rock formations.

In 1973, Chouinard Equipment officially changed its name to

Patagonia, inspired by the pristine and rugged landscapes of the region. With the new name came a renewed focus on producing environmentally friendly products that aligned with the company's values. Patagonia expanded its product line to include a wide range of outdoor apparel, including jackets, fleece, and base layers, all designed with sustainability and performance in mind.

Patagonia's commitment to environmental conservation extends beyond its product offerings. The company has implemented numerous initiatives to reduce its own ecological footprint. Patagonia was one of the first companies to use recycled materials in its products, and it has pioneered innovative manufacturing techniques to minimize waste and energy consumption.

Another integral aspect of Patagonia's ethos is its dedication to activism and using its platform to effect positive change. The company has consistently supported environmental causes and initiatives through its grant program, "1% for the Planet," which donates 1% of its sales to environmental organizations. Patagonia has also been involved in advocacy campaigns, raising awareness about pressing environmental issues such as climate change and public lands conservation.

Patagonia's commitment to social responsibility is evident in its fair labor practices and supply chain transparency. The company actively works to ensure fair wages and safe working conditions for its employees and partners with suppliers who share its values. Patagonia has established a strong reputation for its transparent reporting on labor practices and its efforts to improve working conditions across the industry.

Patagonia's unique approach to business has garnered recognition and accolades. It has been consistently recognized as one of the most socially and environmentally responsible companies. Its founder, Yvon Chouinard, has become a respected figure in the business world and an advocate for sustainable business practices.

The story of Patagonia is not just about creating high-quality outdoor gear but about challenging the status quo and redefining the role of business in society. Through its unwavering commitment to environmental sustainability, ethical practices, and advocacy, Patagonia has become a shining example of how a company can thrive while prioritizing both people and the planet. It serves as an inspiration to others, demonstrating that businesses can be a force for positive change and play a vital role in protecting the environment for future generations.

31. Peloton

The success of Peloton is a motivational example of how fusing technology, fitness, and community can transform at-home exercise. Founded in 2012 by John Foley, Tom Cortese, Hisao Kushi, Yony Feng, and Graham Stanton, Peloton has transformed the way people engage with fitness by bringing immersive, instructor-led workouts directly into their homes.

The idea for Peloton originated from John Foley's frustration with finding convenient and engaging workout options. Recognizing the potential of technology to bridge the gap between gym-quality workouts and the convenience of home exercise, Foley set out to create a connected fitness experience like no other.

The initial product concept centered around a high-quality indoor cycling bike equipped with a large screen that streamed live and on-demand cycling classes led by top instructors. The immersive experience allowed users to join virtual classes, receive real-time performance metrics, and engage with a supportive community of fellow riders from the comfort of their homes.

Peloton's first major challenge was gaining traction in the highly competitive fitness industry. The company started by selling its bikes directly to consumers, combining hardware and software to deliver a seamless fitness experience. To build a community and foster engagement, Peloton introduced social features that allowed users to compete with friends, share achievements, and participate in group challenges.

Peloton's business model also evolved to include a subscription-based service, called the Peloton All-Access Membership. This membership provided unlimited access to the entire library of live and on-demand workouts across various disciplines, including cycling, running, strength training, yoga, and more. This comprehensive approach expanded Peloton's appeal and allowed users to engage in a wide range of workouts without leaving their homes.

As Peloton gained popularity, it continued to innovate and diversify its offerings. In 2018, the company introduced the Peloton Tread, a high-tech treadmill that brought the same immersive experience and community-driven workouts to running enthusiasts. The Peloton App was also launched, enabling users to access Peloton's classes on their mobile devices without the need for specialized equipment.

Peloton's success skyrocketed during the COVID-19 pandemic when gym closures and social distancing measures led to a surge in demand for at-home fitness solutions. The company experienced rapid growth, attracting millions of new customers and expanding its global footprint.

Beyond its hardware and software innovations, Peloton has prioritized building a strong sense of community. The company has fostered a passionate following, with users forming online communities, participating in virtual challenges, and even attending Peloton's in-person events like the annual Homecoming gathering. The instructors have become celebrities in their own right, developing personal connections with their riders and motivating them to achieve their fitness goals.

While Peloton has faced challenges and controversies along its journey, such as safety concerns with its treadmill product line, the company has remained committed to continuous improvement and customer satisfaction. It has invested in research and development, acquiring companies to expand its capabilities and enhance the overall user experience.

Today, Peloton is a household name and a leader in the connected fitness industry. It has successfully merged technology, fitness content, and community engagement to create a comprehensive and immersive workout experience. With its combination of high-quality equipment, instructor-led classes, and a vibrant community, Peloton has redefined the way people approach fitness, making it more accessible, convenient, and enjoyable for individuals of all fitness levels.

The story of Peloton showcases the power of innovation, technology, and community in transforming the fitness industry. By leveraging cutting-edge technology, delivering engaging content, and fostering a supportive community, Peloton has inspired millions to prioritize their health and well-being, setting new standards for home fitness and reshaping the future of exercise.

32. Pinterest

Pinterest's origin is a story about the transformative potential of the visual discovery process. Founded in 2010 by Ben Silbermann, Evan Sharp, and Paul Sciarra, Pinterest has grown into a global platform that allows users to discover, save, and share ideas through visual content.

The idea for Pinterest originated from Ben Silbermann's passion for collecting and organizing items of interest. He recognized the potential of creating a platform that would enable users to curate and share their interests visually. Silbermann believed in the power of images to spark inspiration and wanted to build a tool that would make it easier for people to discover and save ideas online.

In the early stages, Pinterest faced challenges gaining traction and attracting users. The founders focused on refining the platform's features and user experience to make it intuitive and visually appealing. They also worked diligently to build a community of early adopters who would help spread the word about the platform's unique value.

One key factor in Pinterest's growth was its emphasis on the visual aspect of content discovery. Users could "pin" images and videos to their virtual pinboards, creating a collection of visual bookmarks that represented their interests, aspirations, and creative ideas. This visual bookmarking system revolutionized the way people organized and shared content online.

As Pinterest gained popularity, it evolved beyond being just a personal bookmarking tool. It became a platform for users to explore and be inspired by a vast array of content, including recipes, fashion, home decor, travel destinations, and much more. Businesses also began to recognize the marketing potential of Pinterest, leading to the introduction of business accounts and advertising features.

To enhance user engagement, Pinterest continuously introduced new features and functionalities. Rich pins were introduced, allowing users to add more context and details to their pins, such as recipes with ingredients or product information for shopping. The introduction of boards enabled users to categorize and organize their pins into specific themes or projects.

The global reach of Pinterest expanded rapidly as the platform attracted users from around the world. International growth was facilitated by localizing the platform, making it accessible in multiple languages and tailoring content recommendations to specific regions.

In recent years, Pinterest has also focused on leveraging its platform for social impact. It has introduced initiatives to combat misinformation, promote positivity, and prioritize user well-being. Efforts have been made to ensure a safe and inclusive environment, with features that allow users to report and block content that may violate community guidelines.

Pinterest's success has been fueled by its ability to tap into people's desire for inspiration and aspiration. The platform has become a go-to resource for users seeking ideas and visual inspiration for various aspects of their lives. From wedding planning to home improvement projects, Pinterest has become a trusted companion for users to discover and save ideas.

As a publicly traded company, Pinterest continues to evolve and innovate. It has expanded its offerings to include features like shopping integration, allowing users to shop directly from pins, and launching the "Today" tab, which provides personalized recommendations and trending content.

The story of Pinterest is a testament to the power of visual discovery and the human desire for inspiration. Through its visually appealing platform, Pinterest has empowered millions of users to explore their passions, discover new ideas, and bring their creative visions to life. With its ongoing commitment to innovation and user-centric design, Pinterest remains a beloved destination for inspiration, connecting people through the art of visual discovery.

33. Robinhood

The financial sector was shaken up and made more democratic by the creation of Robinhood. Founded in 2013 by Vladimir Tenev and Baiju Bhatt, Robinhood set out to revolutionize the way people access and participate in the stock market by making investing more accessible to the masses.

The idea for Robinhood stemmed from the founders' desire to create a platform that would remove barriers to entry and eliminate the high fees associated with traditional brokerage services. They envisioned a platform that would empower individuals to invest in stocks, exchange-traded funds (ETFs), and cryptocurrencies without the need for extensive financial knowledge or substantial capital.

Robinhood's defining characteristic was its commission-free trading model. By eliminating the fees typically charged by traditional brokerages, Robinhood made investing in the stock market more affordable and accessible to a broader range of individuals. This disruption challenged the established players in the industry and caught the attention of both novice investors and seasoned traders alike.

In addition to commission-free trading, Robinhood's user-friendly mobile app played a significant role in its success. The app provided a seamless and intuitive interface for users to manage their investments, monitor stock prices, and execute trades. Its sleek design and simplified approach appealed to a younger demographic, attracting a new generation of investors who were accustomed to mobile-first experiences.

As Robinhood gained traction, it faced some regulatory challenges and criticism. Questions were raised about the company's revenue model, primarily the practice of selling order flow to market makers, which led to concerns about potential conflicts of interest. However, the company defended its approach, stating that selling order flow enabled it to offer commission-free trading while still generating revenue.

Robinhood's growth was fueled by its ability to tap into the rising interest in investing among millennials and Gen Z, who were seeking accessible platforms to participate in the stock market and build their portfolios. The platform's user-friendly design, educational resources, and features like fractional shares, which allowed investors to buy and sell small portions of expensive stocks, further appealed to this demographic.

The GameStop frenzy in early 2021 brought Robinhood into the spotlight once again. As retail investors banded together to drive up the stock price of GameStop, Robinhood found itself at the center of controversy when it temporarily restricted trading in certain volatile stocks. This move was met with backlash from users and critics who accused the company of favoring institutional investors and limiting the freedom of individual investors.

Despite the challenges and controversies, Robinhood's impact on the financial industry is undeniable. It has inspired other brokerages to adopt commission-free trading, ushering in an era of increased accessibility and competition. The company's success has also prompted traditional brokerages to reconsider their fee structures and embrace digital transformation.

Today, Robinhood continues to evolve and expand its offerings. It has introduced features like cash management accounts, options trading, and cryptocurrency trading, further diversifying its product portfolio and attracting a wider user base. The company went public in 2021, marking a significant milestone in its journey.

The story of Robinhood represents a seismic shift in the financial industry, challenging the status quo and empowering individuals to take control of their financial futures. By democratizing investing and making it more accessible, Robinhood has opened doors for millions of people to participate in the stock market, regardless of their background or wealth. Whether it's for long-term investments, day trading, or exploring the world of cryptocurrencies, Robinhood has redefined the way people approach investing, placing financial opportunities at their fingertips.

34. Salesforce

The founding story of Salesforce is a remarkable narrative of creativity, entrepreneurship, and how the customer relationship management (CRM) sector was transformed. Founded in 1999 by Marc Benioff, Parker Harris, Dave Moellenhoff, and Frank Dominguez, Salesforce has become a global leader in cloud-based CRM software and enterprise solutions.

The idea for Salesforce originated from Marc Benioff's vision of creating a new kind of CRM software—one that would be accessible, user-friendly, and operate entirely on the cloud. At the time, traditional CRM systems were typically complex, expensive, and required extensive on-premises infrastructure. Benioff saw an opportunity to disrupt the industry by providing a scalable and flexible CRM solution that could be accessed from anywhere with an internet connection.

To realize his vision, Benioff assembled a talented team and launched Salesforce.com, a cloud-based CRM platform that offered a subscription-based model, eliminating the need for upfront hardware and software investments. This innovative approach democratized CRM, making it more accessible to businesses of all sizes.

Salesforce quickly gained recognition for its intuitive interface, ease of use, and rapid deployment capabilities. It allowed companies to manage their customer interactions, sales processes, and marketing campaigns more efficiently, empowering sales teams to close deals and marketers to engage customers more effectively.

One of Salesforce's key differentiators was its focus on customer success. The company championed the concept of "Customer Relationship Management 2.0," emphasizing the importance of building strong, long-lasting relationships with customers and prioritizing their needs. This customer-centric approach, combined with continuous innovation and regular software updates, propelled Salesforce to become a trusted partner for businesses worldwide.

As Salesforce grew, it expanded beyond CRM and developed a broad portfolio of cloud-based enterprise solutions. The company introduced Sales Cloud, Service Cloud, Marketing Cloud, and Commerce Cloud, providing organizations with end-to-end solutions for sales, customer service, marketing automation, e-commerce, and more. Additionally, Salesforce developed a vibrant ecosystem of third-party applications and integrations through its AppExchange marketplace, enabling businesses to customize and extend the functionality of their Salesforce deployments.

Salesforce's success was further fueled by its commitment to social responsibility and philanthropy. The company pioneered the 1-1-1 model, pledging to donate 1% of its equity, 1% of its employees' time, and 1% of its products to charitable causes. This philanthropic approach not only made a positive impact on communities but also inspired other companies to adopt similar models and give back to society.

Through strategic acquisitions, Salesforce continued to expand its product offerings and market reach. Notable acquisitions include the purchase of companies like ExactTarget (now Salesforce Marketing Cloud), Tableau (now Salesforce Tableau), and MuleSoft, which enhanced Salesforce's capabilities in areas such as marketing automation, analytics, and data integration.

Salesforce's impact on the CRM industry and the business world as a whole has been profound. The company's cloud-based approach revolutionized the software industry, paving the way for other organizations to adopt cloud computing and embrace the concept of software-as-a-service (SaaS). Salesforce's success also fueled the growth of the broader ecosystem of cloud-based enterprise solutions.

Today, Salesforce is a global powerhouse, serving businesses of all sizes across industries. Its platform has evolved into a comprehensive suite of tools and applications that empower companies to manage customer relationships, streamline operations, and drive growth. The company's commitment to innovation, customer success, and social responsibility continues to shape the future of CRM and cloud computing.

The story of Salesforce exemplifies the transformative power of a bold vision, relentless innovation, and a customer-centric approach. Through its cloud-based CRM solutions, Salesforce has empowered businesses to connect with their customers in new and meaningful ways, driving productivity, growth, and customer loyalty.

35. Shopify

The Shopify story is one of entrepreneurial empowerment, e-commerce democratization, and online retail decentralization. Founded in 2006 by Tobias Lütke, Daniel Weinand, and Scott Lake, Shopify has become a leading global e-commerce platform, enabling individuals and businesses of all sizes to start, grow, and manage their online stores.

The inception of Shopify can be traced back to Tobias Lütke's own experience as an entrepreneur. In 2004, Lütke wanted to launch an online store to sell snowboards, but he found the existing e-commerce platforms to be cumbersome and limited in functionality. Fueled by his frustration, Lütke set out to create a better solution— one that would be easy to use, flexible, and customizable.

Lütke, along with Daniel Weinand and Scott Lake, developed an e-commerce platform initially for their own online snowboard shop, Snowdevil. However, they soon realized that their platform had the potential to empower other entrepreneurs and businesses seeking to establish an online presence. Thus, Shopify was born.

The founders focused on creating a platform that would remove the barriers to entry in e-commerce, making it accessible to anyone with a product to sell. Shopify offered a user-friendly interface, comprehensive features, and customizable design templates, enabling users to set up their online stores quickly and without the need for extensive technical expertise.

One key factor in Shopify's success was its embrace of a subscription-based business model. Instead of charging transaction fees, Shopify offered affordable monthly plans, allowing merchants to keep more of their revenue. This approach resonated with entrepreneurs and small businesses, who saw Shopify as a cost-effective and scalable solution for launching and growing their online stores.

As Shopify gained traction, it continually evolved and expanded its offerings. The platform introduced an extensive range of features, including inventory management, payment processing, shipping integrations, and marketing tools, providing users with a comprehensive suite of e-commerce solutions.

Shopify's commitment to user-centric design and seamless user experience played a crucial role in its growth. The platform enabled entrepreneurs to focus on their businesses rather than getting bogged down by technical complexities. Additionally, Shopify fostered a supportive community through its forums, educational resources, and partnerships with third-party developers, creating a vibrant ecosystem around the platform.

In 2015, Shopify launched Shopify Plus, an enterprise-level solution designed to meet the needs of larger businesses and high-growth brands. Shopify Plus offered advanced features, scalability, and dedicated support, attracting established companies seeking a robust and flexible e-commerce platform.

Shopify's impact on the e-commerce landscape has been profound. It has empowered countless entrepreneurs and businesses worldwide, enabling them to reach customers beyond traditional brick-and-mortar boundaries. Shopify has played a significant role in the rise of direct-to-consumer (DTC) brands, providing them with the tools and infrastructure to compete with established retail giants.

Through strategic partnerships and integrations, Shopify has further extended its reach and capabilities. The platform integrates with numerous third-party applications, payment gateways, and shipping providers, allowing users to tailor their online stores to their specific needs and preferences.

In 2015, Shopify went public, marking a significant milestone in its journey. The company's IPO reflected the confidence and trust placed in Shopify as a leader in the e-commerce industry.

Today, Shopify continues to innovate and expand its offerings. It has introduced additional services, such as Shopify Capital, which provides merchants with access to financing, and Shopify POS, a point-of-sale system for offline retail. The platform also ventured into augmented reality (AR) technology, allowing users to visualize products in real-world settings through the Shopify AR feature.

The story of Shopify exemplifies the power of entrepreneurship and technology to transform industries and empower individuals. By creating an accessible, user-friendly, and feature-rich e

-commerce platform, Shopify has revolutionized the way businesses sell online. Its commitment to simplicity, innovation, and a thriving community has made it the go-to platform for entrepreneurs and established brands alike, shaping the future of e-commerce.

36. Slack

The development of Slack is one of innovative thinking, cooperative communication, and rethinking teamwork. Founded in 2013 by Stewart Butterfield, Eric Costello, Cal Henderson, and Serguei Mourachov, Slack has become a leading workplace communication and collaboration platform, transforming the way teams communicate, share information, and collaborate on projects.

The origins of Slack can be traced back to a game development company called Tiny Speck. While working on a massively multiplayer online game called Glitch, the team faced challenges with internal communication and information sharing. However, they developed an internal communication tool called "Slack" to address these challenges, which soon became more popular than the game itself.

Recognizing the potential of their internal communication tool, the team decided to shift their focus and transform Slack into a standalone platform that could help teams across various industries improve their communication and collaboration. In 2013, Slack was officially launched as a product, and it quickly gained attention and traction.

One of the key innovations of Slack was its intuitive and user-friendly interface. Unlike traditional email or chat platforms, Slack organized conversations into channels, enabling teams to create dedicated spaces for specific topics, projects, or departments. This structure allowed for streamlined and focused communication, reducing noise and making it easier for team members to find and access relevant information.

Slack's emphasis on integrations played a crucial role in its success. The platform seamlessly integrated with a wide range of third-party tools and services, such as project management software, file-sharing platforms, and customer relationship management (CRM) systems. This integration capability allowed users to centralize their workflows and access information from various sources within a single platform, enhancing productivity and collaboration.

As Slack gained popularity, it attracted the attention of both small teams and large enterprises. Its flexibility and scalability made it suitable for teams of all sizes, from startups to Fortune 500 companies. Slack's real-time messaging capabilities, file sharing, and search functionality made it a valuable tool for remote teams, distributed workforces, and organizations with multiple offices worldwide.

Slack's growth was fueled by its commitment to continuous improvement and innovation. The company regularly released updates and introduced new features based on user feedback and evolving market needs. These updates included threaded conversations, advanced search capabilities, voice and video calling, and integrations with popular productivity tools like Google Drive and Trello.

In 2019, Slack went public with a direct listing on the New York Stock Exchange, further solidifying its position as a leader in the collaboration software market. The company's IPO reflected the growing demand for more efficient and streamlined communication solutions in the workplace.

Slack's impact on the way teams communicate and collaborate cannot be overstated. It has helped break down silos, fostered transparency, and enabled remote and distributed teams to work together seamlessly. Slack's user-friendly interface, integration capabilities, and focus on improving workplace communication have reshaped the expectations and standards for collaboration tools.

In 2020, Salesforce, a leading customer relationship management (CRM) company, announced its acquisition of Slack, signaling a new chapter for both companies. The acquisition aims to further integrate collaboration and communication into Salesforce's offerings, providing a comprehensive suite of tools for businesses to manage customer relationships and internal operations.

The story of Slack is a testament to the power of recognizing a problem, iterating on a solution, and building a product that revolutionizes an industry. By reimagining workplace communication, Slack has transformed how teams collaborate, fostering a more connected and productive work environment.

37. SpaceX

The tale of SpaceX is one of ambition, creativity, and pushing the limits of space exploration. Founded in 2002 by entrepreneur Elon Musk, SpaceX, short for Space Exploration Technologies Corp., has emerged as a leading private aerospace manufacturer and space transportation company.

Elon Musk's vision for SpaceX was rooted in his desire to revolutionize space technology, make space travel more accessible, and ultimately enable the colonization of Mars. With a background in entrepreneurship and a successful track record in the technology industry, Musk assembled a team of talented engineers and set out to disrupt the space industry.

The early years of SpaceX were marked by significant challenges and setbacks. The company faced numerous failed launches, including the devastating loss of their first three rockets. However, Musk's unwavering determination, along with his commitment to innovation and cost reduction, propelled SpaceX forward.

In 2008, SpaceX achieved a major milestone when its Falcon 1 rocket became the first privately funded liquid-fueled vehicle to reach orbit. This success brought attention and credibility to the company, positioning it as a serious player in the space industry.

One of SpaceX's defining achievements came in 2012 with the launch of the Dragon spacecraft. SpaceX became the first privately-funded company to send a spacecraft to the International Space Station (ISS) and successfully return it to Earth. This milestone marked a turning point in the commercialization of space exploration and solidified SpaceX's position as a key player in the field.

The breakthrough that truly transformed SpaceX and the space industry came with the development of the Falcon 9 rocket and the creation of the Dragon spacecraft's upgraded version, the Dragon 2. The Falcon 9 became the world's first reusable orbital rocket, capable of delivering payloads to space and then landing back on Earth for reuse. This achievement represented a significant leap forward in reducing the cost of space travel and making it more sustainable.

In 2020, SpaceX achieved another historic milestone with the successful launch of the Crew Dragon spacecraft, carrying NASA astronauts to the ISS. This marked the first crewed mission to be launched from American soil since the retirement of the Space Shuttle in 2011 and restored the United States' capability to launch astronauts independently.

Additionally, SpaceX has made remarkable progress in the development of the Starship spacecraft, designed for long-duration space travel and the eventual colonization of Mars. The Starship represents a giant leap in rocket technology, aiming to be the most powerful and fully reusable spacecraft ever built. SpaceX has conducted multiple test flights of prototypes, pushing the boundaries of engineering and paving the way for future human space exploration.

Beyond its achievements in space exploration, SpaceX has also made significant contributions to the field of satellite communications. The company's Starlink satellite constellation aims to provide global broadband internet coverage, especially to underserved areas. By launching thousands of small satellites into low Earth orbit, SpaceX seeks to revolutionize connectivity on a global scale.

The impact of SpaceX extends far beyond technological advancements. The company's emphasis on cost reduction and reusability has driven competition and innovation in the aerospace industry, forcing traditional players to reevaluate their approaches and accelerate their own development efforts.

SpaceX's success has also revitalized public interest in space exploration and reignited a sense of wonder and inspiration. Elon Musk's vision of making humanity a multiplanetary species has captivated the imagination of people worldwide, fostering a renewed enthusiasm for space travel and the possibilities it holds for the future.

The story of SpaceX showcases the power of audacious goals, relentless innovation, and unwavering determination. By challenging the status quo and pushing the boundaries of what is possible, SpaceX has transformed the space industry and brought us closer to a future where space travel and exploration are within reach for all of humanity.

38. Square

The success of Square serves as a testament to technology's ability to radically alter established businesses. Founded in 2009 by Jack Dorsey and Jim McKelvey, Square has become a leading financial technology company, empowering businesses of all sizes to accept electronic payments and manage their operations seamlessly.

The inception of Square can be traced back to a moment of frustration. Jim McKelvey, a glassblower, lost a sale because he was unable to accept credit card payments. Recognizing the need for a simple and accessible payment solution, McKelvey approached Jack Dorsey, the co-founder of Twitter, with the idea of creating a mobile payment system.

Together, Dorsey and McKelvey set out to build a revolutionary device that would allow anyone with a smartphone or tablet to accept credit card payments. The result was the Square Reader, a small device that plugged into the audio jack of mobile devices, transforming them into portable payment terminals.

Square's launch in 2009 disrupted the traditional payment industry by democratizing card acceptance. Small businesses and individuals who were previously excluded from accepting electronic payments due to high costs and complex requirements now had a simple and affordable solution at their fingertips.

One of the key factors that contributed to Square's success was its focus on user experience and simplicity. Square created an intuitive and user-friendly mobile app that accompanied the Square Reader, enabling businesses to easily accept card payments, track sales, and manage inventory. The user-centric design and seamless experience resonated with merchants, making Square a preferred choice for payment processing.

As Square gained traction, it expanded its product offerings and services to meet the evolving needs of businesses. The company introduced Square Register, a full-featured point-of-sale system for brick-and-mortar stores, and Square Capital, a service that provides small businesses with access to financing based on their transaction history.

Square further diversified its offerings by launching additional services such as Square Invoices, Square Appointments, and Square for Restaurants, catering to the specific needs of different industries. The company's commitment to continuous innovation and its ability to adapt to market demands solidified its position as a comprehensive provider of financial tools and services.

In 2015, Square went public with an initial public offering (IPO), further establishing itself as a prominent player in the fintech industry. The IPO reflected the confidence of investors in Square's disruptive business model and its potential to reshape the way businesses transact and manage their finances.

Over the years, Square expanded its reach beyond payments processing. In 2018, it obtained a BitLicense, allowing it to offer Bitcoin trading capabilities through its Cash App. This move showcased Square's willingness to embrace emerging technologies and explore new avenues in the financial landscape.

Square's impact extends beyond payment processing and financial services. The company has actively contributed to empowering small businesses and entrepreneurs through initiatives like Square Capital and Square Reader SDK, which allows developers to build custom solutions on top of Square's platform.

Square's innovative approach has not only transformed the way businesses accept payments but also democratized access to financial services, enabling economic opportunities for individuals and businesses that were previously underserved or overlooked.

The story of Square exemplifies the power of disruptive innovation and the ability of technology to reshape entire industries. By providing accessible and user-friendly financial tools, Square has empowered millions of businesses to thrive in the digital age. With its commitment to simplicity, innovation, and inclusivity, Square continues to revolutionize the way we transact and manage our finances.

39. Stripe

The success of Stripe is a testament to the value of streamlining complicated procedures and giving companies the tools they need to succeed in the digital economy. Founded in 2010 by Irish brothers Patrick and John Collison, Stripe has emerged as a leading global payments technology company, revolutionizing the way online businesses accept and manage payments.

The journey of Stripe began when Patrick and John Collison recognized the challenges faced by businesses in accepting online payments. They observed that the existing solutions were complex, time-consuming, and lacked a seamless user experience. With a vision to make online transactions easier and more accessible, the Collison brothers set out to build a modern payments infrastructure.

The initial focus of Stripe was on providing developers with a simple and powerful platform to integrate payment processing into their websites and applications. They aimed to simplify the complex world of online payments by creating a unified API (Application Programming Interface) that could handle various payment methods, currencies, and security protocols.

By offering a developer-friendly solution, Stripe quickly gained popularity among startups and developers who were seeking an easy-to-integrate payment system. The company's emphasis on documentation, robust developer tools, and exceptional customer support set it apart from the competition.

One of the key innovations introduced by Stripe was its approach to handling complex payment processes behind the scenes. Rather than requiring businesses to establish relationships with multiple banks and payment processors, Stripe acted as a single point of contact, handling the intricacies of payment processing on behalf of its customers. This simplified the onboarding process and reduced the burden of compliance and regulatory requirements for businesses.

Stripe's commitment to innovation extended beyond payment processing. The company introduced additional services and features to enhance the overall customer experience. These included tools for fraud prevention, subscription management, and global expansion, enabling businesses to scale and adapt to evolving market demands.

As Stripe continued to expand its product offerings, it gained traction among businesses of all sizes, from startups to enterprise-level organizations. Its reputation for reliability, security, and scalability attracted partnerships with major companies such as Shopify, Lyft, and Salesforce, further solidifying its position in the market.

The global nature of Stripe's platform allowed businesses to accept payments from customers around the world, breaking down barriers and enabling seamless international transactions. This global reach, combined with its focus on user experience and developer-friendly infrastructure, contributed to Stripe's rapid growth and widespread adoption.

Over the years, Stripe has continued to innovate and expand its services. The company introduced Stripe Atlas, a program designed to help entrepreneurs start and scale their online businesses by providing them with the necessary tools, guidance, and legal infrastructure. Stripe also launched Stripe Connect, a solution that enables marketplaces and platforms to facilitate payments between buyers and sellers.

The success of Stripe has not gone unnoticed. The company has attracted significant investment and financial backing, with notable investors recognizing its disruptive potential in the payments industry. Stripe's valuation has soared, solidifying its status as one of the most valuable fintech companies globally.

Stripe's impact extends beyond payments. Its focus on empowering businesses, streamlining processes, and fostering innovation has helped shape the digital economy. By removing barriers to online commerce and providing a robust payments infrastructure, Stripe has enabled countless entrepreneurs and businesses to thrive in the digital age.

The story of Stripe demonstrates the transformative power of simplifying complex processes and providing seamless payment solutions. With its customer-centric approach, commitment to innovation, and global reach, Stripe continues to redefine the way businesses transact online and lays the foundation for the future of digital payments.

40. Tencent

The story of Tencent is a remarkable journey of growth, innovation, and diversification, establishing it as one of the world's most valuable technology conglomerates. Founded in 1998 by Pony Ma (Ma Huateng), Tencent has become a powerhouse in the Chinese tech industry, with a wide range of products and services that have shaped the digital landscape in China and beyond.

Tencent's early beginnings can be traced back to its instant messaging platform, QQ, which was launched in 1999. QQ quickly gained popularity, becoming one of the most widely used messaging apps in China, with features such as chat, online gaming, and social networking. This laid the foundation for Tencent's subsequent expansion into various sectors of the digital ecosystem.

One of Tencent's pivotal moments came in 2004 with the launch of its online gaming platform, Tencent Games. It introduced games like "CrossFire" and "League of Legends" to the Chinese market, propelling Tencent to the forefront of the gaming industry. Tencent's strategic investments in both domestic and international game developers and publishers further solidified its position as a global gaming giant.

In addition to gaming, Tencent expanded its portfolio by venturing into social media with the introduction of WeChat (known as Weixin in China) in 2011. WeChat started as a messaging app but evolved into a comprehensive social platform, offering features such as voice and video calls, mobile payments, mini-programs, and more. WeChat's immense popularity in China and its integration of various services transformed it into an indispensable part of daily life for millions of users.

Tencent's success also stems from its strategic investments and acquisitions. The company has actively sought opportunities to expand its reach and diversify its business portfolio. It has made significant investments in various tech companies, both in China and internationally, including stakes in companies like JD.com, Spotify, Snap Inc., and many others. These investments have allowed Tencent to tap into new markets and leverage synergies between different platforms and services.

The company's expansion has not been limited to gaming and social media. Tencent has ventured into areas such as fintech, cloud computing, entertainment, online advertising, artificial intelligence, and autonomous driving. It has launched services like Tencent Music, Tencent Video, Tencent Cloud, and Tencent AI Lab, among others, further solidifying its position as a diversified technology conglomerate.

Tencent's innovative mindset and commitment to continuous improvement have propelled it to the forefront of technological advancements. The company has invested heavily in research and development, focusing on areas such as AI, big data analytics, and cloud infrastructure. It has also fostered collaborations with leading universities and research institutions to stay at the forefront of technological innovation.

The global impact of Tencent is undeniable. Its products and services have touched the lives of billions of people worldwide. Tencent's influence extends beyond its domestic market, with investments and partnerships that have helped drive the growth of various tech companies globally.

However, Tencent has also faced challenges and scrutiny along its journey. As a prominent player in the tech industry, it has encountered regulatory and public concerns related to issues such as user privacy, data security, and market dominance. Tencent has taken steps to address these concerns and comply with regulations, working to enhance transparency and strengthen user protection measures.

The story of Tencent embodies the rapid evolution of the Chinese tech industry and its emergence as a global powerhouse. Through its innovative products, strategic investments, and commitment to technological advancement, Tencent has transformed the digital landscape and established itself as a leading force in the global technology sector. With its focus on innovation and its ability to adapt to changing market dynamics, Tencent continues to shape the future of the digital world.

41. Tesla

The success of Tesla is a testament to the auto industry's need for constant innovation, daring, and the quest of a sustainable future. Founded in 2003 by a group of engineers, including Martin Eberhard and Marc Tarpenning, and later joined by entrepreneurs like Elon Musk, Tesla has become synonymous with electric vehicles and renewable energy solutions.

Tesla's journey began with a grand vision to accelerate the world's transition to sustainable transportation. The company's first major milestone came with the launch of the Tesla Roadster in 2008, an all-electric sports car that showcased the potential of electric vehicle technology. The Roadster, based on a modified Lotus Elise, demonstrated that electric cars could be high-performance, stylish, and capable of long-range travel.

However, it was the introduction of the Tesla Model S in 2012 that truly transformed the perception of electric vehicles. The Model S was an all-electric luxury sedan with impressive range, cutting-edge technology, and stunning design. It quickly gained critical acclaim, earning accolades for its performance, safety features, and its ability to challenge traditional gasoline-powered luxury sedans.

Tesla's success continued with the launch of the Model X, an all-electric SUV, and later the Model 3, a more affordable electric sedan aimed at the mass market. The Model 3 proved to be a game-changer, becoming one of the best-selling electric vehicles worldwide and bringing electric mobility to a broader audience.

One of the key factors that set Tesla apart from its competitors was its commitment to building a robust charging infrastructure. Tesla invested heavily in the development of its Supercharger network, enabling long-distance travel and reducing range anxiety for electric vehicle owners. By strategically deploying Supercharger stations worldwide, Tesla significantly improved the practicality and convenience of electric vehicles.

Beyond its electric vehicles, Tesla expanded its scope to address the broader challenges of sustainable energy. In 2015, the company unveiled the Tesla Powerwall, a home energy storage solution that aimed to revolutionize the way households consume and generate electricity. The Powerwall, combined with Tesla's solar energy products, allowed homeowners to harness renewable energy, store it, and use it at their convenience, reducing dependence on the traditional power grid.

Tesla's impact extended beyond the automotive and energy sectors. The company's relentless focus on innovation and technological advancement pushed the boundaries of what was considered possible in the industry. Tesla's Autopilot feature, an advanced driver-assistance system, showcased the potential for autonomous driving and set the stage for the future of transportation.

Moreover, Tesla's bold vision for sustainable transportation and its commitment to open-sourcing its patents further demonstrated its dedication to driving industry-wide change. By making its intellectual property accessible to other companies, Tesla aimed to encourage the development of electric vehicles and accelerate the transition away from fossil fuels.

Tesla's success has not come without challenges. The company faced numerous hurdles, including production bottlenecks, financial pressures, and skeptics questioning the viability of electric vehicles. However, Tesla's ability to innovate, iterate, and continually improve its products enabled it to overcome these obstacles and maintain its trajectory toward success.

Today, Tesla stands as a global leader in the electric vehicle market, with a strong brand, a loyal customer base, and a robust ecosystem that includes charging infrastructure, energy products, and software innovations. Its impact on the automotive industry and the transition to sustainable energy is undeniable, inspiring other manufacturers to embrace electric mobility and reshape the future of transportation.

The story of Tesla is one of audacity, disruption, and a relentless pursuit of a sustainable future. Through its innovative electric vehicles, cutting-edge technology, and commitment to sustainable energy solutions, Tesla has redefined the automotive industry and sparked a global movement towards cleaner and more efficient transportation.

42. Twitter

Twitter's history demonstrates the potential of brevity, real-time communication, and social media innovation. Founded in 2006 by Jack Dorsey, Biz Stone, and Evan Williams, Twitter has grown to become one of the most influential social networking platforms, connecting people around the world through short, 280-character messages called "tweets."

The origins of Twitter can be traced back to a previous project called Odeo, a podcasting platform. When Apple announced the integration of podcasting into iTunes, Odeo faced an uncertain future. In response, Jack Dorsey, one of Odeo's engineers, proposed the idea of a short messaging service that would allow people to share their status updates with a small group of followers.

With the support of Biz Stone and Evan Williams, the concept quickly gained traction, and in March 2006, Twitter was officially launched. Initially, the platform was intended for internal use within Odeo, but it soon became evident that Twitter had the potential to be much more than a side project.

Twitter's breakthrough moment came during the 2007 South by Southwest (SXSW) Interactive conference, where the platform garnered significant attention and usage. The ability to send short, real-time updates to a wide audience struck a chord with users, and

Twitter's popularity skyrocketed. People started using Twitter to share news, thoughts, opinions, and engage in conversations, effectively creating a new form of social communication.

As Twitter gained momentum, it underwent several significant milestones and developments. The introduction of features like hashtags (#) and retweets allowed users to organize and share content more effectively, amplifying the reach and impact of tweets. Celebrities, politicians, and influencers began using Twitter as a platform to engage with their audiences directly, further fueling its growth and cultural relevance.

Twitter's impact on real-time news and information dissemination became particularly evident during events such as natural disasters, political movements, and major global events. The platform became a vital source for breaking news, citizen journalism, and public discourse, empowering individuals to share their perspectives and participate in global conversations.

The platform's simplicity and focus on brevity became its defining characteristic. With a strict character limit initially set at 140 characters (later expanded to 280 characters), Twitter encouraged concise and impactful messaging. This constraint fostered creativity, succinctness, and encouraged users to craft their messages thoughtfully.

Twitter's influence and cultural significance led to its widespread adoption worldwide. It transcended geographic boundaries, language barriers, and demographics, connecting people from diverse backgrounds and facilitating conversations on a global scale. It became a platform for activism, social movements, and community building, enabling users to unite around shared interests and causes.

Over the years, Twitter has continued to evolve and introduce new features to enhance user experience and address emerging trends. It incorporated multimedia content, allowing users to share photos, videos, and GIFs. The introduction of Twitter Moments provided a curated overview of the most significant events happening on the platform. Twitter also made efforts to combat harassment and improve user safety by implementing stricter policies and tools to report and prevent abusive behavior.

Twitter's influence has extended beyond individual users to encompass businesses, brands, and public figures. It has become an essential tool for marketing, customer engagement, and real-time brand communication. Companies leverage Twitter to reach and interact with their target audiences, gather feedback, and stay connected with industry trends.

Despite its success, Twitter has faced challenges along its journey. Monetization has been a recurring issue, with the company experimenting with various advertising models to generate revenue. It has also grappled with issues of misinformation, hate speech, and the spread of harmful content, leading to ongoing efforts to enhance content moderation and user safety.

The story of Twitter is a testament to the power of simplicity, real-time communication, and the ability of

a concise message to have a profound impact. With its unique format and global reach, Twitter has revolutionized social media and transformed the way we connect, share information, and engage in public discourse. As it continues to evolve and adapt to changing user needs, Twitter remains a vital platform shaping the digital landscape and enabling people to have a voice in the global conversation.

43. Uber

Uber's journey is one of disruptive innovation, revolutionizing the transportation sector and changing how people navigate urban environments. Founded in 2009 by Travis Kalanick and Garrett Camp, Uber has become synonymous with ride-hailing, connecting passengers with drivers through a convenient mobile app.

The idea for Uber was born when Garrett Camp struggled to find a cab in Paris during a snowy evening. He envisioned a service that would allow people to request a ride with a few taps on their smartphones. Joined by Travis Kalanick, the duo launched UberCab (later renamed Uber) as an upscale black car service in San Francisco.

Uber's breakthrough came with the introduction of its innovative business model. Unlike traditional taxi services, Uber utilized the power of technology to connect riders with drivers, providing a more efficient and seamless experience. The mobile app allowed users to request a ride, track the driver's location, estimate fares, and make cashless payments, revolutionizing the way people accessed transportation services.

Uber quickly expanded to other cities, attracting both riders and drivers with the promise of convenience and flexible earning opportunities. The company's rapid growth was fueled by its ability to scale quickly and adapt to local market needs. It also offered various service tiers, such as UberX (affordable rides in everyday vehicles) and UberPOOL (shared rides), catering to a wide range of transportation preferences.

As Uber gained popularity, it faced regulatory challenges and opposition from traditional taxi industries and local governments. Critics argued that Uber operated in a gray area, not subject to the same regulations as traditional taxi services. These disputes led to legal battles and debates around issues such as driver classification, safety, and fair competition.

Despite these challenges, Uber's impact on the transportation industry was undeniable. The convenience, affordability, and flexibility offered by the platform resonated with millions of users worldwide. It transformed the way people thought about transportation, making ridesharing a mainstream option and challenging the dominance of traditional taxis.

Uber's success led to the introduction of additional services. UberEATS, launched in 2014, allowed users to order food from local restaurants for delivery. Uber Freight, launched in 2017, connected shippers and carriers in the trucking industry. Uber also ventured into electric bikes and scooters with acquisitions and partnerships, further expanding its presence in the micro-mobility space.

However, Uber's journey has not been without controversies. The company faced criticism and scrutiny over issues such as safety concerns, privacy, treatment of drivers, surge pricing, and corporate culture. In response, Uber has taken steps to address these concerns, implementing safety features, improving driver benefits, and working towards a more inclusive and responsible business model.

Uber's impact extended beyond its core ride-hailing business. It inspired the emergence of the "gig economy," where individuals could work flexibly as independent contractors. Uber's success paved the way for the rise of other ride-hailing and mobility platforms globally, transforming urban transportation around the world.

Over the years, Uber has continued to evolve and diversify its offerings. The company invested in autonomous vehicle technology, aiming to revolutionize transportation further. It also expanded its presence internationally, entering new markets and adapting its services to local needs and regulations.

The story of Uber exemplifies the power of innovation and technology in disrupting traditional industries. By leveraging the convenience of mobile apps and the sharing economy, Uber revolutionized transportation, empowering individuals and transforming the way we think about getting from point A to point B. As it continues to navigate the challenges of regulation, competition, and public perception, Uber remains a prominent force shaping the future of transportation and mobility.

44. Wayfair

The Wayfair story is one of e-commerce innovation, upending the home furnishings market, and reinventing how consumers browse for furniture and home goods. Founded in 2002 by Niraj Shah and Steve Conine, Wayfair has grown to become one of the largest online destinations for home goods and furnishings.

The idea for Wayfair was born out of the founders' frustration with the limited options and high prices they encountered while shopping for furniture. They recognized an opportunity to leverage the power of the internet to offer customers a vast selection of products at competitive prices, all conveniently accessible from the comfort of their homes.

Initially, Wayfair operated under the brand name CSN Stores, which stood for Conine and Shah's initials. The company began as a collection of niche online stores, each specializing in a specific product category such as furniture, home decor, and lighting. By offering a diverse range of products and catering to different customer needs, Wayfair aimed to become a one-stop-shop for home furnishing and decor.

In 2011, CSN Stores rebranded as Wayfair, a unified brand that encompassed all its niche online stores. The new name reflected the company's vision of creating an exceptional shopping experience focused on the needs and desires of homeowners.

Wayfair's success can be attributed to several key factors. First, the company invested heavily in building a robust e-commerce platform and a user-friendly website. The intuitive interface, advanced search capabilities, and comprehensive product information made it easy for customers to browse and find exactly what they were looking for.

Second, Wayfair implemented a unique drop-shipping model, which allowed the company to offer an extensive product catalog without the need for maintaining massive inventory. This approach enabled Wayfair to partner directly with manufacturers and suppliers, ensuring a wide selection of products while minimizing operational costs.

Third, Wayfair prioritized customer service and satisfaction. The company established a dedicated customer service team that provided personalized assistance, answered product-related questions, and addressed any concerns promptly. Wayfair also implemented a generous return policy, instilling confidence in customers and mitigating the perceived risk of purchasing furniture online.

Wayfair's growth was fueled by strategic acquisitions and expansions. The company acquired several online retailers, such as AllModern, Joss & Main, and Perigold, to broaden its product assortment and cater to different customer segments. Additionally, Wayfair expanded its international presence, entering new markets and adapting its offerings to suit local tastes and preferences.

The company's marketing efforts played a significant role in driving brand awareness and customer acquisition. Wayfair invested in digital marketing, leveraging social media, search engine optimization, and targeted advertising to reach a broad audience. The company also sponsored home improvement and design shows, further solidifying its position as a go-to destination for home furnishings.

Wayfair's impact on the home furnishing industry cannot be overstated. It challenged the traditional brick-and-mortar retail model, offering an extensive online catalog, competitive prices, and the convenience of doorstep delivery. By leveraging technology and data-driven insights, Wayfair disrupted the industry, creating a new standard for online furniture shopping.

However, Wayfair's success has not been without challenges. The company faced scrutiny over labor practices, supply chain transparency, and pricing controversies. Critics also argued that the company's aggressive expansion and heavy marketing spending contributed to financial losses.

Nonetheless, Wayfair has continued to innovate and adapt to evolving customer needs. The company has embraced augmented reality (AR) and virtual reality (VR) technologies, allowing customers to visualize furniture in their homes before making a purchase. It has also invested in data analytics and artificial intelligence to enhance personalization and provide tailored recommendations to customers.

Today, Wayfair remains a prominent player in the e-commerce industry, offering a vast selection of furniture, decor, and home goods

to customers worldwide. Its commitment to innovation, customer-centricity, and convenience has solidified its position as a leader in the online home furnishing market, shaping the way people design and furnish their living spaces.

45. Waymo

Waymo's history is one of technology advancement, self-driving cars, and the search for more reliable and effective transportation. Waymo, formerly known as the Google Self-Driving Car Project, is a subsidiary of Alphabet Inc., Google's parent company. It was founded in 2009 with the goal of developing autonomous vehicle technology that could revolutionize the way we travel.

The roots of Waymo can be traced back to the Stanford University's Stanford Racing Team, which participated in the DARPA Grand Challenge in 2005 and the DARPA Urban Challenge in 2007. These competitions aimed to accelerate the development of self-driving technologies. Several members of the Stanford team, including Sebastian Thrun, Chris Urmson, and Anthony Levandowski, later joined Google and became key figures in the development of autonomous driving technology.

In 2009, Google launched the Google Self-Driving Car Project, with the aim of building a fully autonomous vehicle that could safely navigate public roads. The project's early prototypes used modified conventional vehicles equipped with an array of sensors, cameras, and advanced software to perceive and interpret the surrounding environment.

The Google Self-Driving Car Project made significant strides in autonomous vehicle technology, conducting extensive testing on public roads in various locations. By 2012, their vehicles had logged hundreds of thousands of miles, showcasing promising results in terms of safety and reliability.

In 2016, the project evolved into Waymo, a standalone subsidiary under Alphabet Inc. This transition reflected the growing maturity and focus on commercializing autonomous driving technology. Waymo's mission expanded beyond building self-driving cars to becoming a leading provider of autonomous transportation solutions.

Waymo's approach to autonomous driving combines various technologies, including advanced sensors, machine learning algorithms, and high-definition mapping. Their vehicles use lidar (light detection and ranging) sensors, radar, and cameras to perceive the surrounding environment, allowing them to detect and respond to pedestrians, vehicles, and other objects on the road.

One of Waymo's key milestones came in 2015 when they conducted the first fully autonomous ride on public roads in Austin, Texas. This demonstration showcased the potential of self-driving technology and its ability to navigate complex urban environments safely.

Waymo's efforts have also focused on refining its technology for ride-hailing services. In 2018, Waymo launched the Waymo One autonomous ride-hailing service in the Phoenix metropolitan area, making it the world's first commercial self-driving taxi service. This marked a significant step toward their vision of creating a safer, more accessible, and more efficient transportation system.

Waymo's advancements have not been without challenges. The company has faced technical hurdles, regulatory complexities, and public skepticism surrounding the safety and feasibility of autonomous vehicles. However, Waymo's commitment to rigorous testing, collaboration with regulatory bodies, and a focus on safety has helped address these concerns and build public trust.

Beyond ride-hailing, Waymo has expanded its partnerships and collaborations. It has collaborated with automakers such as Jaguar Land Rover and Chrysler to integrate its self-driving technology into their vehicles. Waymo has also engaged in partnerships with logistics and delivery companies to explore autonomous trucking and last-mile delivery solutions.

As of now, Waymo continues to innovate and refine its autonomous driving technology. The company has accumulated millions of autonomous miles on public roads and continues to expand its testing and deployment efforts. Waymo's ambition is to unlock the potential of self-driving technology, transforming transportation by improving road safety, reducing traffic congestion, and enhancing mobility for individuals worldwide.

The story of Waymo represents the relentless pursuit of a future where autonomous vehicles play a central role in transportation. Through pioneering technology, rigorous testing, and strategic partnerships, Waymo is at the forefront of shaping the autonomous driving industry and paving the way for a new era of mobility.

46. WeWork

WeWork's history is one of a bold idea, quick growth, and a sharp rise and fall in the co-working sector. Founded in 2010 by Adam Neumann and Miguel McKelvey, WeWork aimed to revolutionize the way people work by providing flexible and collaborative office spaces for freelancers, startups, and established companies.

WeWork started with a single co-working space in New York City, offering shared workspaces, amenities, and a sense of community. The concept resonated with entrepreneurs and small businesses seeking an alternative to traditional office leases. WeWork's vibrant and stylish work environments, coupled with networking opportunities and events, attracted a growing number of members.

The company's initial success led to rapid expansion, both domestically and internationally. WeWork secured significant investments and partnerships, fueling its growth and establishing a global presence. By 2019, WeWork operated in over 100 cities around the world, boasting a valuation of tens of billions of dollars.

WeWork's business model was built on leasing large office spaces from landlords, designing them with trendy aesthetics, and subleasing them to individuals and companies. The company aimed to create a "community" within its workspaces, fostering collaboration and a sense of belonging among its members.

Under the leadership of Adam Neumann, WeWork pursued an ambitious vision of becoming much more than a co-working space provider. The company expanded into various ventures, including WeLive (co-living spaces), Rise by We (wellness centers), and WeGrow (an educational program). It also launched WeWork Labs, an incubator and accelerator program for startups.

However, WeWork's rapid expansion and ambitious goals were accompanied by mounting concerns. The company faced scrutiny over its financial health, as it incurred substantial losses year after year. Questions were raised about its valuation, corporate governance, and the sustainability of its business model.

In 2019, WeWork's plans to go public revealed deeper issues. The company's initial public offering (IPO) was met with significant skepticism from investors and analysts, who questioned its valuation, governance practices, and ability to generate sustainable profits. Amid mounting scrutiny, Adam Neumann stepped down as CEO, and WeWork's IPO plans were shelved.

The subsequent months saw a dramatic turn of events for WeWork. SoftBank, a major investor, intervened with a rescue package to prevent the company's collapse. As part of the bailout, WeWork underwent significant restructuring, including cost-cutting measures, leadership changes, and the divestment of non-core businesses.

The story of WeWork represents both the potential and pitfalls of the co-working industry. The company played a pivotal role in popularizing the concept of flexible workspaces and community-driven environments. It brought together entrepreneurs, startups, and established companies under one roof, fostering collaboration and innovation.

However, WeWork's rapid expansion and lofty ambitions led to significant challenges. Its financial struggles, governance issues, and leadership controversies brought to light fundamental flaws in its business model and corporate culture. The episode served as a cautionary tale for startups and investors, highlighting the importance of sustainable growth, transparency, and sound governance practices.

Despite the setbacks, WeWork continues to operate and provide co-working spaces to individuals and businesses. The company has undergone significant changes, focusing on core operations and profitability. It aims to rebuild trust and deliver on its original promise of providing flexible and inspiring workspaces for its members.

The story of WeWork serves as a reminder of the complexities and risks inherent in the startup world. While it faced significant challenges and had to recalibrate its trajectory, WeWork played a pivotal role in reshaping the modern workplace and inspiring the broader co-working industry to evolve.

47. WorkDay

Workday is a modern success story that exemplifies innovation, resilience, and the power of disruptive ideas. Founded in 2005 by Aneel Bhusri and Dave Duffield, Workday set out to revolutionize the world of enterprise software and human capital management (HCM).

The story of Workday begins with Aneel Bhusri, a former executive at PeopleSoft, a leading enterprise software company. Following the acquisition of PeopleSoft by Oracle in 2004, Bhusri, along with his former colleague Dave Duffield, saw an opportunity to reimagine the way organizations manage their most valuable asset— their people.

Bhusri and Duffield aimed to create a cloud-based, user-friendly, and comprehensive HCM solution that would replace the outdated and cumbersome on-premises systems prevalent at the time. They believed that the future of enterprise software lied in the power of the cloud, providing organizations with greater agility, flexibility, and real-time insights.

With a clear vision in mind, Bhusri and Duffield founded Workday in 2005, setting up their headquarters in Pleasanton, California. They assembled a team of talented engineers and industry experts, and together they embarked on the mission to reinvent

HCM software from the ground up.

The early years were challenging for Workday. The team faced intense competition from established players in the enterprise software market. However, Bhusri and Duffield remained steadfast in their commitment to building a best-in-class, cloud-based HCM platform.

In 2007, Workday released its first product, Workday Human Capital Management, which offered organizations a unified system to manage various aspects of their workforce, including HR, payroll, talent management, and more. Workday's user-friendly interface, real-time analytics, and mobile capabilities set it apart from traditional enterprise software solutions.

As the market recognized the value of Workday's innovative approach, the company started gaining traction. Workday's client base began to grow, with organizations across industries embracing the platform's simplicity, scalability, and ability to adapt to changing business needs.

Workday continued to expand its product offerings, introducing solutions like Workday Financial Management to transform the way companies manage their finances. The company's commitment to constant innovation and customer satisfaction propelled its success, leading to significant growth and recognition in the industry.

In 2012, Workday went public with a highly successful initial public offering (IPO) that raised over $700 million. This milestone marked a testament to the company's market position and investor confidence in its vision.

Over the years, Workday expanded its global footprint, serving organizations of all sizes, from small businesses to multinational corporations. Today, the company continues to innovate, adding new features, functionalities, and modules to its platform, enabling organizations to navigate complex workforce challenges and drive business growth.

Workday's success story is a testament to the transformative power of disruptive thinking, technological innovation, and a relentless focus on customer value. The company's commitment to reimagining enterprise software and human capital management has not only reshaped an industry but also empowered organizations to better manage their most critical resource—their people.

As Workday continues to evolve and shape the future of enterprise software, its story serves as an inspiration for entrepreneurs and innovators who dare to challenge the status quo and strive to create meaningful change in the world.

48. Xiaomi

The success of Xiaomi is a fascinating narrative of inventiveness, speed, and ascent in the global technology sector. Founded in 2010 by entrepreneur Lei Jun, Xiaomi set out to create high-quality, feature-rich, and affordable smartphones for the mass market.

Lei Jun, often referred to as the "Steve Jobs of China," envisioned Xiaomi as a company that combined cutting-edge technology with a user-centric approach. Inspired by the success of companies like Apple, Lei Jun aimed to bring a similar level of craftsmanship and user experience to Xiaomi's products while making them accessible to a broader audience.

Xiaomi's early years were marked by its unique business model, often described as an "Internet company with a hardware focus." Instead of relying solely on hardware sales for revenue, Xiaomi emphasized its ecosystem of internet services, software, and content, which provided additional revenue streams and enhanced user engagement.

The company's first smartphone, the Xiaomi Mi 1, was launched in 2011. It garnered significant attention and popularity in China due to its attractive price point, robust specifications, and customized Android-based operating system known as MIUI. Xiaomi adopted an online sales model, bypassing traditional retail channels and selling directly to consumers through its website, which helped reduce costs and fostered a sense of community among Xiaomi users.

Xiaomi's "Mi Fan" community played a crucial role in the company's success. Through online forums, social media, and frequent interaction with users, Xiaomi actively engaged its customers, sought feedback, and incorporated their suggestions into product development. This fan-centric approach not only created a loyal customer base but also generated substantial word-of-mouth promotion for the brand.

The company's product portfolio expanded rapidly beyond smartphones. Xiaomi ventured into various consumer electronics categories, including smart TVs, smart home devices, wearables, and other Internet of Things (IoT) devices. Xiaomi's ecosystem approach aimed to create an interconnected network of devices that seamlessly worked together, providing a unified user experience.

International expansion was a key part of Xiaomi's growth strategy. The company initially focused on emerging markets, such as India, Southeast Asia, and parts of Europe. Xiaomi's affordable yet feature-rich smartphones resonated with consumers in these markets, quickly establishing the company as a leading player.

Xiaomi's success in global markets was also fueled by its online-focused sales model, aggressive marketing strategies, and the establishment of local partnerships and production facilities. The company's ability to adapt its products and services to suit the preferences and needs of different markets played a significant role in its international growth.

While Xiaomi's rise has been impressive, it has not been without challenges. The company faced intense competition from both domestic and international rivals, particularly in the highly competitive smartphone market. Xiaomi also encountered intellectual property disputes and regulatory hurdles as it expanded into new territories.

In recent years, Xiaomi has expanded its reach beyond hardware and embraced a broader ecosystem approach. It has further diversified its portfolio, offering a range of products and services, including cloud services, fintech solutions, and content platforms. Xiaomi's ecosystem strategy aims to create an interconnected digital lifestyle for its users, providing seamless integration across devices and services.

Today, Xiaomi is one of the world's largest smartphone manufacturers and a prominent player in the global consumer electronics market. The company's commitment to delivering innovative and affordable products, its fan-centric approach, and its ecosystem strategy have been instrumental in its success.

The story of Xiaomi showcases the power of disruptive business models, customer-centric innovation, and a relentless drive for affordability and quality. As Xiaomi continues to expand its presence globally and explore new technologies, it remains a force to be reckoned with in the ever-evolving technology landscape.

49. Xpeng Motors

The history of Xpeng Motors is a testament to the electric vehicle (EV) industry's explosive growth and innovation in China. Founded in 2014 by entrepreneur He Xiaopeng, Xpeng Motors, also known as Xiaopeng Motors, aims to become a leading player in the development and production of smart electric vehicles.

Xpeng Motors emerged at a time when the EV market in China was gaining significant traction and government support. He Xiaopeng, with a background in technology and entrepreneurship, recognized the potential of electric vehicles to revolutionize transportation and reduce carbon emissions.

The company's early focus was on developing smart, connected electric vehicles with advanced autonomous driving capabilities. Xpeng Motors aimed to deliver a seamless integration of technology, artificial intelligence, and innovative design in its vehicles, providing a differentiated and user-centric experience.

Xpeng Motors' first vehicle, the Xpeng G3, an all-electric SUV, was unveiled in 2018. The G3 quickly gained attention for its competitive pricing, extensive range, and advanced features, including a voice-activated assistant, facial recognition, and over-the-air software updates.

In 2019, Xpeng Motors launched its second model, the P7, a premium all-electric sedan. The P7 boasted an impressive range, cutting-edge autonomous driving features, and a sleek design. The vehicle received positive reviews for its performance, technology, and overall driving experience.

Xpeng Motors positioned itself as a technology-driven company, investing heavily in research and development to enhance its electric vehicle offerings. The company established its own research and development centers, collaborating with leading global suppliers and partners to develop advanced EV technologies and improve battery efficiency.

Xpeng Motors also leveraged artificial intelligence and data analytics to enhance its autonomous driving capabilities. The company's fleet of test vehicles collected vast amounts of data, enabling continuous improvement in its autonomous driving algorithms and systems.

To support its growth and expansion, Xpeng Motors secured significant investments from prominent investors, including Alibaba Group, IDG Capital, and Xiaomi Corporation. These investments provided the company with the necessary capital to accelerate its manufacturing capabilities, expand its sales and service network, and invest in further technological advancements.

Xpeng Motors also made strategic partnerships with key players in the industry. In 2020, the company formed a partnership with Guangzhou Automobile Group (GAC) to jointly develop and manufacture electric vehicles. This collaboration aimed to leverage GAC's manufacturing expertise and Xpeng Motors' technology to enhance their competitive edge in the market.

In terms of market expansion, Xpeng Motors focused on the domestic Chinese market initially. It established a strong presence in major cities, building a network of direct sales stores and service centers to cater to customer needs. The company also invested in charging infrastructure development, collaborating with third-party charging providers to ensure convenient access to charging stations for its customers.

In 2020, Xpeng Motors took a significant step towards international expansion by launching its electric vehicles in Norway, marking its first entry into the European market. This move demonstrated the company's ambition to compete on a global scale and expand its customer base beyond China.

As of now, Xpeng Motors continues to innovate and expand its product lineup. The company unveiled its third model, the Xpeng G3i, in 2020, targeting the mid-range SUV market. Xpeng Motors also has plans to launch additional models, including a larger SUV and a sedan, to cater to different customer preferences and market segments.

The story of Xpeng Motors exemplifies the remarkable growth and innovation in the Chinese EV industry. With its focus on smart, connected electric vehicles and advanced autonomous driving technology, Xpeng Motors aims to transform the future of mobility and provide sustainable transportation solutions. As the company continues to push boundaries and expand its global footprint, it remains poised to shape the future of the automotive industry.

50. Zoom

Zoom revolutionized the way people connect and communicate. Founded in 2011 by entrepreneur Eric Yuan, Zoom emerged as a leading video conferencing platform that transformed the landscape of remote communication and collaboration.

Eric Yuan, a former executive at WebEx, had a vision to create a video conferencing solution that would provide a seamless and high-quality user experience. He believed that video communication should be easy, reliable, and accessible to anyone, regardless of their location or device.

Zoom's journey began with a focus on delivering a superior user experience. The company invested heavily in developing its own video and audio technology, prioritizing reliability and crystal-clear audiovisuals. Zoom's platform offered high-definition video conferencing, screen sharing, and interactive features that made remote meetings feel more immersive and collaborative.

One of the key differentiators of Zoom was its emphasis on simplicity and ease of use. The platform was designed to be intuitive and user-friendly, allowing participants to join meetings with a single click and navigate the interface effortlessly. This simplicity resonated with users, making Zoom a preferred choice for both personal and professional communication.

In its early years, Zoom targeted businesses and enterprises as its primary customer base. The platform's scalability, flexibility, and cost-effectiveness appealed to organizations of all sizes, enabling them to conduct virtual meetings, webinars, and training sessions with ease. Zoom's ability to accommodate large numbers of participants in a single meeting without sacrificing performance set it apart from competitors.

However, Zoom's true breakthrough came in 2020 with the global outbreak of the COVID-19 pandemic. As millions of people around the world shifted to remote work and virtual communication became the new norm, Zoom experienced a dramatic surge in popularity and usage. Its user base grew exponentially, as individuals, businesses, schools, and even governments relied on Zoom to stay connected during the unprecedented times.

Zoom's adaptability and responsiveness during the pandemic were critical to its success. The company quickly expanded its infrastructure to handle the increased demand, enhanced security measures, and introduced features specifically tailored to remote collaboration, such as virtual backgrounds, breakout rooms, and live transcription.

Despite its meteoric rise, Zoom faced challenges along the way. The sudden surge in usage brought attention to privacy and security concerns. The company responded swiftly by implementing additional security features, updating its encryption protocols, and engaging in regular dialogue with users and privacy advocates to address the issues and strengthen user trust.

Zoom's success and impact extended beyond the corporate world. The platform became an essential tool for remote education, virtual events, and social gatherings, enabling people to stay connected and engaged despite physical distancing measures. It played a crucial role in maintaining human connections and facilitating communication in a time of isolation and uncertainty.

The story of Zoom showcases the transformative power of

technology to bridge distances, foster collaboration, and revolutionize communication. With its commitment to simplicity, reliability, and user-centric design, Zoom has become a household name and a symbol of remote work and digital communication.

As the world continues to evolve, Zoom remains at the forefront of innovation, constantly improving its platform, introducing new features, and exploring opportunities to enhance the virtual communication experience. The company's ongoing success highlights the significance of seamless connectivity and the increasing importance of video conferencing in our interconnected world.

Other Titles You Might Enjoy:

The Empowered Entrepreneurs Series
   50 Founders Stories
   50 Innovative Companies
   20 Ways to Use AI In Your Small Business

Income Builders Series
   Start With $0: Unleashing the Power of Internet Money
   50 Side Hustle Ideas for Australians
   Make Money Grow on Trees

A Business Leaders Guide To
   50 IT Concepts for Business Leaders
   50 Operations Concepts for Business Leaders
   50 Legal Concepts for Business Leaders
   50 Economics Concepts for Business Leaders
   50 Finance Concepts for Business Leaders
   50 HR Concepts for Business Leaders
   50 Management Concepts for Business Leaders
   50 Marketing Concepts for Business Leaders
   50 Sales Concepts for Business Leaders
   50 ESG Concepts for Business Leaders
   100 Frameworks & Concepts for Business Leaders

The CEO's Playbook Series

   The Diversity, Equity & Inclusion Playbook
   The Recession Playbook
   The Branding & Reputation Playbook
   The Artificial Intelligence Playbook
   The Future of Work Playbook
   The Web3, Metaverse and Virtual Reality Playbook
   The Mastering Client Engagement Playbook
   The Cybersecurity and Cybercrime Playbook
   The Climate Crisis Playbook
   The 21st Economy Playbook

About the Author

Daniel Boyd is an accomplished business strategist, thought leader, and author specializing in guiding business leaders towards innovative and effective decision-making. With over two decades of experience in the corporate world, Daniel has honed his expertise in various industries, ranging from technology to finance and beyond. He is known for his deep understanding of business dynamics and his ability to distill complex concepts into practical frameworks that drive organizational success.

Daniel's passion for empowering business leaders to think critically and strategically has led him to write a range of books in the business niche. Drawing on his extensive experience and research, Daniel presents a comprehensive collection of frameworks and concepts that equip leaders with the tools they need to navigate the complexities of the business landscape.

When he is not immersed in the world of business, Daniel enjoys spending time with his family, exploring new cultures through travel, and indulging in outdoor activities that rejuvenate his mind and inspire his creativity.